TANYA TURTON

Copyright © 2021 Tanya Turton

Copyright remains the property of the author
and apart from any fair dealing for the purposes
of private study, research, criticism or review, as
permitted under the Copyright Act, no part may be
reproduced by any process without written permission.
All inquiries should be made to the author.

Typeset & Cover by Chain of Hearts Creative

National Library of Australia - ISBN-978-0-6452064-2-5

"WE ARE A BELIEF
UNTO OURSELVES
TO BE ALWAYS
A WILLINGNESS
TO BE".

In this is always you.

INFINITE PROCESS WITHIN US ALL

Would it not be correct to ask, in the questioning of oneself to be seeing this that they are of what it appears as to be the absolute truth, for of this you are.

For we are all into this that we are to be seen in absolute knowing of the far outreaching magnificent that we hold ourselves as you into this that we see to be the whole, the complete the ONE. In your choosing of these to be your words of description to speak of us to be, we stand correct within this that you speak.

In ones curiosity to become one will always seek to find the truth that is to reside within in such respect for this that you are to be seen always in our eyes to suggest of truth that we be. There is never nor will be another of this uniqueness that you express to be, for you are all in your own entitlement to be seen as this of highest regard in this that you be.

We are the ever-benevolent beings of light-based enthusiasm that you be to us to see and reside into. It is out of immense respect shown by you that we are to feel this entitlement that you are as us to be ever present within you to express, to experience, to reside into this exactness that you see.

In ones understanding of the process or the deliberate intent that you would speak of to be, it is in this so choosing of this extraordinary self to become that you did. You outlined all expectations in many to ask, to believe into this birthing to see yourself into this that you felt as correctness within you to explore. For you are the great adventurer of this life and of the many as so chosen as yours to become into and it was of this understanding within self to be recognised into that you were the asker of more to be realised within to discover.

All opportunities have been granted in your request in which it was that you called forth to ask, it was to have been a innerness of knowing that is realised upon ones completion or shall we offer here the successful completion of the previous life just exited out of that has guided you to an even greater receiving of growth, evolving and learnings to be, that you felt this urge rising again from within the etherical being of light that you stand so deeply embedded into, that you felt confident in this love of self to ask again for another journey or life to be present into as.....

the next instalment shall we offer here to speak of it as a way to understand ones progress from an earthly aspect of this one to be.

You have transcended into many formats of this deliberate interaction of oneself to see yourself as many recognitions and aspects of this to be viewed into to know of this that is you to always be deliberate in one's inner knowing of complete being that you are to request of this that you are to know. One's evolvement is very much intended as to be always asked, offered, and given, for you are the truest decider as you are here upon this planet today to see yourself into, to be the holder of the real asker of this that you are wanting to be.

In one's progression or processing of exactness it is to be felt as a non-description of this that one would seek to see of this that we are. For our presence is felt in many ways to speak of it as such and this would be to respond to the many interactions that are to be offered up to us shall we say to ask of this connection to be felt. In one's ability to be deliberately sensing in this self to feel of us, a suggestion to offer as a rhythm of movement and momentum would be an exact consideration of this that we be to be felt into.

The progression to be felt into, is one of a deliberateness that we feel the need to speak about and do here in this now to hear, for it is often in many that one's ability to feel of the progression to proceed further into a sense of self to be worthy of self-growth and of a desiring to be able to wish of themselves to be seen as more, will always be a stopper of sorts or blockage to ones innate ability that is; if let be, the true hearer to feel of this that you really are to be seen as in one's ability to become Intune shall we offer this to hear as a suggestion one must be in the process of self-willingness to understand and to accept all that is to appear from within to be presented.

In my willingness to see, I shall.

One's path is deliberate; YES, and in this we are to offer, maybe hard to comprehend or believe this we hear often and yet it is in this willingness to feel this to know, that one will recognise that they are ready once again to come into a realisation spoken as.

Simply spoken;

You are far greater than ones such as yourselves have ever let yourselves imagine.

This view of us that we see.

It is of us in this ALL that we chose to represent as a voice to be heard by many in their so choosing of us to be known by them to speak, to hear into. WE are many this you are to know and our sensing of ourselves to be is correct in all appearances of which it is that we appear into. WE are ever present in all offerings to be seen into, we offer only a nondescript formation to be explained as of what it is that we are of; the simple reasoning to be explained is that we are not of a format that ones such as you have ever experienced before or will ever know into this human life. Your insisting to the what and how and ifs to be required always in a deliberate hesitation to not trust of self to see correctly. If it cannot be seen by the human eye than, {this disagreeance within to suggest is to hold all humans that ask back from truly receiving} We speak of it as this simple statement to hear:

I CAN NOT SEE, SO I DON'T.

Correct, in all ways to be received as right within.

If you cannot see or think as not able; you will not. It is not the seeing that is of absolute importance to us to be spoken of, but more so the feeling of this genuineness in ones heartfelt space as a certainness to know this as a truth being spoken of us, by you as us to be received.

WE are absolute; and you, in many have heard of us being described of in this way. We are absolute, for we see of ourselves in no other way other than complete, yet complete within one's ability to be always of the other or essences of this that we are to be seen as complete within them. There is no hesitation or sense of not to be in this absolute knowing of truth that we are to be recognised fully within the all that is to be accepted in our righteousness to be ever felt as truth, justice, and honesty in an openness that is to respond to the all of eternity to be seen into as ours as yours.

Many explanations have been offered as to of how I am to view you.

What would you suggest as the truth in me to see you as?

In ones requiring of their own truth to be asked, felt, or heard within another is a deliberate intent of this 'HUMAN'.
YES! humanly spoken it is yet to become apparent to the many that are asking or have asked, and this includes you that they are to feel us eventually as the correct line of connection or recognition to flow through from us in you, as yourself to be 'I'.

It is in the many that are to be ever present in us for all reasons beknown to us as theirs in choice to be speaking of us as. Let us say here to speak; that not one is incorrect or correct for all improvisations or offerings are absolute to the relevant speaker in this, their now that they reside into. We are not of one to be a willingness to be seen in a particular way, so we offer no solid indications as to what we are to look like, or sound like, or appear as. It is in this formless, limitless and ever-ness that is truly our way in which it is that we present.

So, in the suggesting of this to be, we become the all that is.

We ask you here to bravely and courageously feel this that we are, interpret us to be your understanding of this that we be to you. For you are the ever-shining brightest ray to us it appears and not of another to be heard, {for all voices are heard and seen YES! this we offer}, but it is of your light that is the important one in this to be felt as your truth. You are to ask and see, to receive and know that this that you think; is correct within you. Your truth is wise, bold, correct and ever knowing for you.

NEVER OF ANOTHER,
ARE YOU TO LIVE INTO.

This is your truth as we know of it to be,

Can we offer this to be heard, that in the choosing of us to be present, you will feel the **GREAT** within you to rise. This great, yes is us, but know of this to be spoken, that this is YOU. Always held deeply in a non-complacent view of self to be seen, for you are the true seer in all senses to be experienced into and of this it is that we are to know you in this exact moment that you present to be, that you are always heard, received, and loved by us as
'I'.

We see **TRUTH** as a viable word of justice, respect, and faith to be held into by those of you that know of this to be a word in your language to be spoken of in this way. See of us as this, a righteousness within the confounds of this that we stand into, and it is never that you are held so tightly by the human form that you cannot find a strength from within to be released from the thinkers way or mind to be willing to accept any truth to be heard as yours or not. One is to be ever present in this that is spoken by others or self to ask constantly,

"Is this my truth or belief"
Feel that this is okay to be received by you as a question??? This is and should be a requirement or request by you to allow it to rise, to be asked, to be heard.

Delve deeper into these ones that they are, to think as of them to be the trusted speakers surrounding you, to be speaking your TRUTHS in this that you think.

You are to accept this truth in us as yours.

Feel not of a sadness when it sits heavy into you to ask, **is it their truth or my own.** Many it is we see and experience into, are known as an important part of all understandings in this that you are whole to be, and in this we have witnessed many acceptances, beliefs, conversations, and interpretations offered to ones such as you in human formation present in this place or moment of your NOW as to question or query your truths to be known to you as yours or not.

ASK! dear one we speak; so that you may hear only your truths spoken by us in you.

Would you suggest this to be a good place to stand into to ask?

YES, in all that you are to appear to us to be in this your Now of which it is that you are feeling these responses within you as to the opening from within to ask....

THEN YOU SHALL.

Know that this is the place where many connections and realignments are felt within, many walls are torn down or built even, many offerings or beliefs are to be acknowledged, dissected, and maybe thrown out the window shall we offer, in regard to the how, what and why of your life's impressions or presumptions of truths and beliefs to appear suddenly confronting you, asking you to speak to them, recognise, hear and assess them.

Let this be a great period of suggestion for you to wallow into, to rejoice into, to feel a sensing of fear into, to view yourself in a rawness that one has not seen, to feel a sense of loss or disrespect even to the thoughts that are to rise as to being so gullible or trusting of others. It is not to say that all that is and has been offered to you to be spoken as has been incorrect or wrong, for let us say that there are many that are well meaning in their suggestions of thoughts in all aspects to be, kindness and love is offered by many that we see, and often many truths are to be seen by us as correct, but let all this that you ask to be questioned, to be a response within you to feel to find your way to your righteousness that is to be your truth to know as yours.

We speak of this that one must be always in a willingness to be seeing of themselves as their truth and in all formatting of this that you are to feel this first and foremost in regard to overrule shall we say of what you are advised or hearing into.

Suggestion to be offered; One is to always feel correct into this that one is to be, knowing that what they feel is to be their north pointing compass needle to be always guiding them home inwardly shall we say, as to be correct in response to the voice that they are to hear as theirs. This voice of love is yours and will not steer you wrong but it is in a lack of FAITH and TRUST that one often does not allow it to be recognised as a truth within you, recognition to know this voice and that you will never feel the need to stop and adjust this gauge within to be seen correct, for you are always in ever a truthful part of us to be.

You speak deeply and convincingly of Truth, why?

When one is to be feeling from within a rising to ask or an uncertainty it would appear as to what or who it is that they are and to do/ or be in this life.

It is in this small moment that one will feel to stumble, or fall and felt within as a sensing that there must be more. It is to surely rise, in this we know to speak, that in just this glimpse of self to be a query to ask, one will interpret of all that they are to sit into as to be a question of their truths to be contained in a place of doubt, to second guess, judge oneself and request to not ask of more.

This we speak, stay steady as this is to rise and felt as needed to be asked, for you are not alone as we offer to you to hear that many have fallen as have or will you, many have doubted all that they thought or are thinking to be truths, many have felt lost and deceived by not only themselves but others, many have felt the need to be questioning into all this that they are to know.

BUT IN THIS WE SPEAK WITH A GRANDNESS IN OUR WORDS, this is your discovering of this truly magnificent you to be felt and seeing into.

GET READY!

This is your **TRUTH** unravelling from all that you hold deep within as truths to be told, felt, witnessed, observed, and heard as your own.

In this space of which it is that one is to remember to feel a sense of recognition within that is right and is almost to be felt as a knowing then in this it is that you are to feel as the correctness that you are and in here it is that your faith in you is to grow, opening a path to be founded from within in all aspects that you are to shine into as you deliberate in this very being of existence to be . Here is the TRUTH that you need to be present into for you will hear no other speak these words for you in this way that you do.

BE bold in this that you are to hear as correct, for you may never need to feel the urge to utter this that you know as sacred within you, but you will know this that we speak of to you that you are correct in every aspect that you be to speak this as your truth of us to be. For you are this truth that you seek, that you see, you are of us in truth to be, this that you are you.

You speak of truth as strength and certainty, I AM still to feel this rise within myself as a correctness to speak.

OUR sweet ones that you are, you will this we are to express as our truth within you to feel. You will be in a sense of certainness, knowing and of grand self-worth to cherish from within. Invade you it will, into all organs, cells, thoughts, and presence to be, with such intensity to be felt that you will not need ever to look externally outwardly of you or to others, for you will know and in this we wish to offer....

It will come, in a strength & certainty to be spoke {surprisingly to some}, this voice of LOVE will be felt in the most extravagant way to you, for it will be your truth to speak, to hear of and no one feels it like you.

CHAPTER 1

TO KNOW OF THIS THAT YOU ARE.

We speak in only grandness of you, for you are to be of us. Is it not?

It is to appear that in ones asking of us to be it is to become apparent to all that you see that you are to be more in the asking of what it is that you see.

Can we offer here to speak; that it is entirely of us that you be equipped into all aspects of this that we are in absolute knowing that we are you to be.

We are carrying the greater part of you still to be spoken of within us to be seen in this that we be. We sense of your innerness to know, to speak of all in this that you seek to be. Your experiences and desiring of this you that you are to be, was taken into a consideration of all that you in us are to hold dear. You asked with the greatest of intentions to be seen into this way to appear, you stood strong in your words to ask to be of this in intent to strive within this self to be of an asking to become. You sought into all reasoning's and suggestions to be of this want to establish deeply within to be able to ask in this your very now to be of this wanting to know of this,

WHO AND WHAT IS IT THAT I AM?
(TO BE OR BECOME)

When this reverence within this self is felt to rise to be uncovered or questioned to be heard, it is in this space of oneself to be felt as to ask this question. WHO or WHAT is it that I am? Let all that is in need to be heard be spoken, for of this you are to know it will in many ways appear to you. You are gifted and guided intuitively it is to be spoken of and in this unveiling within, you will steadily poke along in a sense of self to be found. Cherish into all aspects of this one that you are present into to be asking to be found. She has been hidden deeply for a while it appears and upon the releasing or de-clothing of this that you are, will be felt as a desire to be asked. You will feel into many unique places of self to be trying, not all paths of reveal are pleasant this we know and in this we agree that they are in the requesting by you to be. So, do not despair or give up for it will feel like corruption from within to begin, mistrust as a word it has been offered to us to be heard, dissatisfaction then overtakes as what it is that I am to become, urgency and lack of patience grips you like no other, fear is prominent into of what it is that you cannot see or understand.

We are to offer this again, you have all stood in this place before, in many moments of self to reflect, to discover to be enabling of this human that you are to rediscover this love that beams so loudly from within to be heard, it is just that you have forgotten. And in this we speak, we can confirm, you will find of us again for we are not lost to you it is just this form that has forgotten again as she/ he has undertaken this journey as theirs to be revealed and you will find this YOU again to be heard, for she has never left you nor will she/ he ever do.

I AM hearing these words spoken often by many, WHY?

> In these words you are to speak knowingly as confidence, trust, faith, bold, magnificence, but most importantly we are to offer LOVE.

THIS IS CORRECT, YES! it is in many that are starting to choose to listen to the love that they are within, and it is the opening in many that are to find themselves in this place to ask. For you see, it is the changing from within, that this reconnection to one's soul that you be, that you so choose of this space to be yours to ask. Many like you, are to be standing in this place that you appear to stand, and they too are wanting more to see, to know, even to remember of this that they are. For you see it can only stay hidden by most for so long before the word of love is to be realised as in this that you BE, and it is to spread from you to another in often not even their knowing of this that you are to emit, it is contagious of this it is to say and all that feel you in this particular way will respond in time of this to be their own to know that they will want to feel of this love to be their very own.

We do not need to be an offeror here to the many that ask for this uniqueness that you are established so profoundly from within. This you as unique, we hold dear within us, and is ever present within all that is seen or not. So, it is not in any doubt to be spoken of that you all will feel of this that we are to rise to be heard in your desiring to ask of it to be mine.

If it is invisible this love that you speak in a certainty as, how is it that it is so powerful?

Much is to be spoken here in these great words of LOVE, has it not been of yours to cherish into this life upon this in humanly form to feel of a love so grand by self.
It is of this simple place to stand that in finding this love within self to be heard as no greater love than is to be felt, that you the receiver of this love will turn to face us in the deepest desire to become. The many of you that are feeling again these feelings of love to be spoke will know of the way in which you are to face to stand, for you will see that our love; *this love of one* is all around and there is no direction that you in this physical could stand that you will not feel this love to be so grand. When it is known to you as us to be you, you will need not to speak to seek this love

in that of another for your love will shine to the heavens and above in such a powerful way that all that see of you will know that you have found your way. To be shining so bold in a clarity of this that you do to be this that you are, you will meet of the many that are to be singing their light proudly, so embrace all that you are present in to see and they too will be of this light that you be, united always in this one unique LOVE, that we speak of as this that we BE YOU.

In a powerful way it is that we offer to speak of this that we have heard many to voice, for the force you are to find sitting within is a directness that is to become all correct within you, and that will often overwhelm ones that have sat quietly spoken as the owner of this voice that has appeared as wanting not to speak or be heard. We offer; this is a recognition within you to be heard, receive this voice as powerfully yours, fulfilled and driven by your truths of this that you see yourself to be.

IN power becomes strength, in power becomes confidence, in power also lays ego>>> Yes this we see to know, but in the true sensing of your power to be the driver of this that you have stepped into you will know that POWERFUL this Love is to be and this love that you are to have established within you in so many faucets to see you will know the difference between ego to speak to offer its power in comparison to the feeling of love to be the power that you are to feel. Never doubt of your power within you to be known, for it will fill you in this entirety that you be, over lapping and extruding from within that you will feel this love in such a powerful way to be that you will be a confident, considerate gentleness to show kind and compassion to all that you see. It will not need be a force of brut or admiration that one is to need if anything it will be quite the opposite to be shown by thee. You are this equipped light of love to be eternally centred into this that we are ALL to be a part of; The One, The ALL that is to be, so rejoice in all that is to flow for you in this right place, feel to know that you are POWERFUL IN THIS LOVE TO BE YOURS TO SEE YOURSELF AS TRUTH.

How can we be all so divinely held in this place of LOVE, are there not too many?

In this human to ask this question to be then yes one would have trouble it would seem to see of this place that we be to hold so many of you that you be in this earthly form to be to suggest.

Know dear ones that you are not of this where it is that we are and in this it is to get heavy to hear for the most that are to ask. Your existence is constant in all that you be, you are neither here nor there it is to be knowing to us to speak. You are deliberate yes, it is to feel in this form that you be to see, but your willingness to feel of this earthly touch to experience is one that you have achieved, know that you are to be seen as primitive if to compare in eyes to see as us. Be felt not judged as a simple yet basic existence in this density needed to become upon this planet earth as it is to be seeming to be. One such as you in this journey of self to evolve for it was of the greater one within that you decided into this that you would become.

In the ability to be seeing of self to be this that you are not, one can and will start to be realising of this that the ALL that be ever present within the all that you see and the all that you do not is really of what it is that you are.

TO hold into this form here is a must to experience all this that this planet has offered to you to think in to as what it is that one is to need. WE in you accepted this to be yours to discover.

So, achieve into everyday that you feel yourself present within for there was much in your asking of self to be here to ask to be experienced by this that you be.

We are compelled here to offer that not all that you know will make sense or be understood by this mind as to be the asker in most cases to be spoke. But know that you will feel to become an acceptance within the all that you be willing by most to have become. You seek deeply to ask to be receiving more of this it is to know, but in an intuitiveness that you are all to be holding deeply within. She knows all this that we are and all that you will ask. You are tied into all eternity it is to be spoken of here to be yours to know.

Be deliberate in your asking of this to know that you are the chosen of the all that are 'her' to become and in your rightness within you knew that you would feel this request to know within to rise, but you were willing within this self to be asked to know and you will see often it appears by most to ask always of more to know. Deliberate you are in the asker of this information to know but until it is that you are to return to the fuller version of you that you will most likely not be the receiver of the absoluteness of this that we are, for it is not likely that the many of you that are to ask can even comprehend of this that we are BUT know this; *it is exactly this that we are that you be.*

Feel this as it is written to be received by this channels interpretation as to be of her own, for you are all to be the informant of self to be so that one can be forth coming in speech, words and inner wisdom that is yours to hold onto to be forever the truth speaker of this that you are to BE.

Many times, in resistance is spent, ones such as you in the human form are to be hidden or restrained into a belief of self to be of this to be another and not truly yours/or their own.

If one were to give self an opportunity to be in a non-judging moment of self to be the writer of all that one seeks to ask,

IS THIS MY BELIEF OR THEIRS?

Here in this moment of truthful expression, I will write to see the truths/beliefs that I have carried as my own. In this my NOW to ASK as in a wanting to feel the answers

to these questions that rise from within.
Let all be spoken from the bearer of my
truths to be spoken so that I may hear
of the correctness that is mine to hear.

BELIEFS…. I CARRY,

I ASK, MINE OR NOT?

(These may be your own, family traditions,
friends or simply just moments captured
by you as a thought to be seen into).
Often it appears that upon ones realising
to begin to ask, much is unwrapped or
unveiled regarding these beliefs, wants
or ideals from who? and why it is that
we are holding/ or living into them.

THIS WE ASK YOU WHY?

THESE ARE MY WRITINGS TO BE FELT FIRST, THEN I WILL HEAR ALL THAT I HAVE WRITTEN.

Why was it so hard to write these words? We hear of you to ask.

In willingness to be heard, one must be of open heart and in a forgiveness of yourself to be revealing of all that is to be offered. It has been a while it appears to be spoken of here in this that you have allowed of yourself to be honest and open and of truth to be speaking. We sense of ones uncertainness to be in this place of which it is to speak to see all this that you are to receive. You are felt to be constricted in old ways of thought and in which to think these are even still current within you today. So, let this self be felt to soften, to be receiving into this that we are to be the silence within you that is safe to sit, to feel of a certain sensing of peace to calm, it is in all endeavours of this to think of yourself as to not be in this place to reveal that you will find yourself to hesitate this we say to offer, it is okay for you will, in an internal determination to be heard. You as are many, are of this quiet voice so hardly heard, not recognised in speech to be yours, it is to feel this opening within that one will be gripped by a sensing of intense knowing of this that you are to reveal to write that this is you. The real you, the true you, the you that is of us to be.

FEEL THIS TO BE
IN ALL YOUR WANTING
TO HEAR,
TO SPEAK,
TO KNOW.

CHAPTER 2

NOW IS YOURS

Of all that one is to see themselves into it is to be this your NOW, so often spoken as to be the exactness that you are. Be deliberate in your conscious awareness of this to be spoken as your most valuable essence within to be seen. For it is of this humanly time to think of as to be not always aware of, for it is to notice, one likes to visit the present and review of the past, this we say is not of the moment that you are to be present within. It is this NOW, this exact moment that you are here to sit. Preview of all that is present in this very aspect of you in this life to live for it is you that we see here to be of the onlyness that is you. You are to be often deprived of this valuable NOW as we offer it to be, for too often your thoughts are distracted in an eagerness or hurriedness to feel elsewhere and not of this that is NOW to be worthy of you to be willing to see. It is of this NOW that one is to cherish, for it is the offeror of the All that you be ever present into, the realness that you are to see as the one space in this very moment of this life to be previewed into that you can call it to be exactly as you are to see you.

You SPEAK of this NOW as if it is IMPORTANT, what if I do not like my now?

It is with great love in a clarity to be felt that one is to only see of this Now, for there are many that do not. And in one's willingness to always be not of this very moment they are to miss so much. The revealing of this self to be seen into is a willing component of the one that holds you tight, seeing only of the one that is not willing to change. To view of this that you are not or not to find joy is to be felt within is it not in a truth to be spoken of as yours that you are to deny. See not to the externalness that you are to witness to investigate to find this that you think of you to be. It is in the seeing of what is within the gentle persuasion from the voice of kind and just that you will become to be a wanting to see into every moment that surrounds you to be.

To live into this moment of choice to know it as you to be, one must have been in a place to ask to hear this that you have tried to find. A place of rest and steadiness to be felt for many have and will endeavour to seek this innermost feeling of love to be yours attached to all that you think, see, and do. In ones hoping to find more than what appears not, you will as we say always be the seer of what it is to be thinking of to be.

So, as we have spoken of in several ways you are the receiver of all that you see, to think, & to be.

In one's ability to be ever present in this very moment of this to be called your NOW, you will start unwillingly at first to be a participant in this more that you will feel present within. It is a change of pace and a difference of view that is required, words spoken are different in the usual way that one would repeat of this to be theirs to hear, you are the asker of this to be yours in a deliberate reasoning from within, for it is this soul that has been participating in your expansion for many moons it would appear, so to be in this understanding that all that you are to receive, is YES! to be seen in a wash of love from within, but to be also seen as an innate truth to be yours to notice that this is YOU.

Space is often given I AM told.
What does this mean?

When one is to speak of or hear into a speaking as such to be a forthcoming or to be opened in a space from within, it is in the sensing of self to be willing to feel and to get to know this righteousness that is you. Space or freedom from thought must always be a receiving of self to be asked, so that one can turn off the thinking mind or the external offerings of this you to be the ever-relevant comprehension of this you that you are.

In ones sensing of this space to become apparent to the seer to see as a place of resistant human to be, let yourself find this space to call your own, no specific set-up or insistent need, just a certainty from within to be feeling an air of nothingness to interpret, for you will grow into this space we are to offer. Start small, feel as not to be incorrect in this that appears, for in this connection, is yours and ours to share, you will soon find that you are everywhere. It is to be sensing an openness to be revealed that you are to no longer feel the need to linger in this reality of this that one feels as earth. You will feel a longing to be filled with a continual asking from this within to be always of this space to be felt as a place of recluse, calm and quiet to linger and in it you shall grow, expanding and experiencing of All this that appears to be not real. YOU are of this space, this observation we say for you are far greater space than you appear not. It is to appear that in the observing of self as just this that you think to be in only human framework to be, you limit yourself in the real version of you to appear as this limitlessness that you really are.

One's space is to become a reasoning within to allow self to see of and all capabilities in which you are. It is in here, this connection that you are seen accomplished of all into this that you are and still must become.

For YOU were aware of all this one is to be residing within freely, non-negotiable, deliberate of intent, wellness and as an honouring of thy self to be truth in all that you accept oneself as is.

It is here that you have grown into to feel of this as an expansion within to be seen as this to know by you as the reality of which it is that you are choosing oneself to be seen into. We are of this ever-knowing sense of self to be, for we have dived deeply into this ones energy or offering as such this that you are to become accustomed with this that is in a recognition that is yours to surpass you into the different realities of which it is that one is to sit into. In one's physical sensing of this that one is to be they will feel to be non-coherent in regard to the greatness that you are and will often be found to dwell into a place as to be not accepting of this space to be found easily within. To choose of this NOW, this space of ones openness as it is to be presented and to become willing in all aspirations that you are to think of to be, this is to become for you a place of acceptance to see this self as more than you have ever dreamed, imagined, or allowed oneself to be thought of as.

NOW....... is an understanding of this present moment to be thought of? Is this correct to ask?

In ones boldness to ask of this to be offered to one in this way YES, it is to become a recognition into this self to be ever always present in this exact moment of awareness to be seen into, for too many it appears to us to witness are in a continual processing of future or further developments or desires to be this that they are not yet to be and are ignorant shall we say to the current NOW.

Embrace this existence into this space to say, you are here now in this that you are to see, deliberate creation of self to become into a vulnerability it appears to be coherent to the willingness to see. It is not to glance quickly over or to ignore of what is, it is this present moment of self to be seeing into that much is to be revealed. For you are this exactness that you be NOW, no need to adjust or correct of what it is that you appear to be.

My current NOW feels limited.

To sit in a space of unrest or despair it would appear that most are to do, to let all that feels as though it is not to be, is where the struggle to be accepting you in this physical form to present, is to feel enough. The deliberate one within is not of this to see and will not feel into this that you are trying to persuade oneself to see as a true reality of this that one sees into. You are the seer of all that is, and in this offering, we say as we have many times before,

> 'The version you see or assume to see as this that you are is truly your asking of them to be whether willingly or not, it is often the thinking mind that is acknowledging this to be of what it is felt or believed as real'. Is it not?

It is in the concept of thought that much is generated to be allowed to be thought of as is, so to feel in this place of limitation, to be stuck, unmoveable is all in line with this sensor(you) to be not feeling enough, for you to see yourself as.

In this one must trust to feel first the initial feelings of this believer inside to say

YES, I AM ENOUGH.... To be able to say this is to want to feel for the speaker of enoughness to be the encouraging words that you are to be responsive to.

Deliberate in words to offer is easier said than done. Is this not? To speak them becomes easy overtime, almost common placed we would say, repetitive YES, but it appears that they are lacking the most valuable part to make them work and this is the sound of HONESTY and GENUITY.

In many, feeling as to lack self-worth and not enough is to overpower many of you in this that we are witness to devalue or degrade the voice that speaks words of encouragement to be heard as not a real need within. You are to always find yourself in this to be your NOW of a position it appears to purposely stand in this space to hear, to feel all this that is to be your NOW of current understanding. YES, it will change in an instance to become of your next NOW to see as yours, in any given moment of such that you BE;

you are the holder of your truth to speak, to be the feeler of all that you feel, the changer of intention to be different, the seer of all that you are seeing to believe as relevant to you.

Feel this statement we speak >>>>>

> You are the holder of this great power or force within; in this ability to be the all that you so seek to see to find. So why not in this very instance of yours to be your NOW would you not allow for the believer of all that is right within you now and always not be allowed to be heard, for she is you. She is all of this that we see as the great creator of initial love to be ever directed into and of you."

So, step into your recognition of this that you are, for you already are all this that is transcendent to see. It is ALL in the eyes of the seer that does or does not believe this is you that you present to the looking glass to be seen into as you.

Of this we ask; How are you showing up for you? How are you choosing to see you?

WE speak gallantly it is of this to offer, that this one that you are to see {in human being} as the holder of all intentions to be felt, the thinker that is, is not to be your ruler, for it is not so. Yes, this human being to think itself is strong, undermining, and resistant to self-help one would offer.

But you in your innerness of love to connect into is where you will find your BOLD & BRAVE voice to speak.

Choosing how I look.

In every day, every moment it is you that chooses, not ever another should this be made theirs to be felt as yours to allow. You are not ever to be viewed through another's eyes, words, or feelings. **YOU JUST ARE NOT.**

Take ownership of this willingness within for she/he is your want to speak, to hear, to feel this that is real *'the real you'* that you are. Let her define all of this that you are. She will not tell tales, in always truth she is to speak. She is only to feel of the greatest love for you and in this you might start to respond. For this love that she/ he and us are to be is where you find the opening of this believer to be hidden so deeply away out of sight. In this acceptance of love to flow, it is of her that you just might try to change your perception or view of this you that you have held onto so tightly to.

WHAT or WHO would I BE if I were not this ME?

WE know the answers that you seek are so deeply yours to find, they will this we say be made prevalent to be in every asking that you speak. IN every moment to trust this that you hear to speak, you will hear your concerns being raised, in the openness of one to trust, you will feel yourself to become a release to be felt even if just as a slowness to start, for it is of this that you are asking to see. **IS IT NOT?**

Your view of you is powerful! It is the reflection of all this that we be that you are to see, so to see of us in this way as not, you must stop. For it is not the image that we are to see. Step away for a moment or close your eyes, if need be, pause awhile in this sensing to see, know this to speak. You are this light that shines so gallantly from within to surround you to fill you complete. This is your NOW that we are wishing you to see. Feel as you intend to speak courageously to be.

> This 'US' we are, is for you
> to see this that you BE.

Hold dearly into ones NOW to speak of it as valuable. You are to see this as a moment in your so time to enter here into love that you speak, this now is relevant only here in this that you choose to speak, feel, or see. Feel its importance for it will not be again, never deliberate in presentation to be this same that it is again. You are the holder of this power, feel as these words are yours to know. You are deliberate seers of all this that be in this exact moment in which you trust. This is your now, your window shall we say that you look into or out of every day, minute, second or moment. So why would you not want to see or ask for a view so grand? For this is your now and it is one upon its passing that you will never see again. So, step into your now. LOVE all that you see and get ready for your next now for it will be even grander than the last, this we speak as true. LOVE your NOW, Live BOLD in your NOW, this NOW is you in TRUTH, Believe this now as you.

OUR MESSAGE TO SPEAK...

We are presence to be felt in all this that is to appear as your NOW to be. Let us be the interpretation of this that you see for all is present within this that you see to know of you and I to be NOW.

BEING PRESENT...

Be ever present in this your NOW, for it is to be the most important space in which it is that you will ever stand to see.

CHAPTER 3

SENSING OF THY SELF TO BE.

I AM.

I AM ME.

I AM ME IN ALL I SEE.

I AM ME IN ALL I SEE IN YOU.

I AM ME IN ALL I SEE IN YOU TO BE.

I AM ME IN ALL I SEE IN YOU TO BE BEAUTIFUL.

In this knowing that I have chosen to sit to recognise this voice that I am to hear speak to me, I know this is **ME**. I feel all willingness in this space to be wanting to be open to receive all suggestions that I may hear spoken or thought, for they are mine to rise to ask and in this I will agree at times YES, I will struggle to hear what I need to hear, and I will feel fearful in what I will feel or see, I will laugh at myself ludicrously in regards to of what I think in here, I will doubt into this that I think or speak, I will struggle to sit, but this I DO KNOW, in here I will GROW.

For All that I commit to, to see and discover to feel I know that this is me, the real me challenging myself in this space and it is this I know that I AM willing to reveal that I AM ME, so I will encourage all of these reasons, feelings and thoughts to rise on up for if it is not me that is willing to see how it is that I became me then HOW will I ever get to know the REAL ME THAT I BE.

Show yourself kind here in this place that you stand for let us say there is no other as grand as this that you show to be. You are deliberate intents to be just as.

Your human characteristics, traits and personalities are all yours to be felt as correct within, they are ones that you have chosen to become, whether planted by self or many along your journey of this life to have become. One is always in a space it feels to be to judge and notice in all that is not right or incorrect this we see to know. It is in this offering that we must ask of you to relinquish all distrust that you show this self to be of, for you are to always offer to yourself to hear in words of I cannot, or I will not, or I am not like most???

This we say that is great for we would not have you any other way, this you that you perceive of yourself to be, is exactly in what it is that we like for it is in this that we see is the you that you so lovingly saw yourself to be, so in saying this, it was this you that you felt the desire to change, to ask, to envision of more to be rise.

A substantial amount of humanly time and energy is spent in self-help, self-doubt, and self-growth it appears to be seen, really the search appears endless to those of us that are to look upon. One if willing must see through all of this to be spoken to be offered for you within your willingness will be placed into this space of which it is to ask, **IS THIS REALLY ME?**

YES, we offer to say. For when ones vision is to be exact and the heart is open wide and you are to feel your thoughts in a forgiving and nurturing way, you will feel this to know that you are exactly as you are meant to be. You'll lose the need to compete, comparison is to become uniquely theirs, you will feel your inner-ness become the driver from within, you will release the need for the voice or opinions of others, you will feel satisfaction in all that you see, your grip loosens on all that you feel the need to grasp onto just in case, you will feel love for yourself and others in a new way, your thoughts become clearer. You will feel lighter, free, and deliberate in this space. You are to know that all that you need is easily received.

Diligently spoken of this you are to speak; for in ones sensing to be they appear to feel lost upon this viewing to see, standing into many or behind those that are not you to be. Wanting not to be heard to speak, for it is of your voice that you have forgotten of all the magic that she holds and is capable to speak. To guide you so definitely she must this you are to know for she has seen your path and planned it like so. Aware she was to all that you chose and in this she is to know. She will not interfere or query of what it is that you appear to utter, even if it is not of what she knows, it is this you that these certain words to hear are your own. You will hear she knows of this; she is sure. Let yourself be easy here, for you are not to know that held within is a voice so proud and brave and correct in all she knows. To feel the human component to subside you will for in all that we see are ready to subscribe to this eternal journal of wisdom that is forever yours to be writing in a continuation of all that you desire. You are the holder of this bold in voice to hear, so let the outer external-ness that you see yourself to be, feel as to disappear as if to fade away. This you, IS ever evolving to become more and your experiences are many to live, speak and to see, so embrace of this chance to hear into these words to say.

'I AM DELIBERATE IN EVERY WAY, THERE IS NO-ONE ELSE LIKE ME'.

CHAPTER 4

CONCEPT OF THOUGHTS, CONCEIVING IDEAS.

Interception within self to become.

You are all to be witness to the removal of thoughts as to not, for these are the energy blocks within that are to expel all encouragement and forwardness to be yours to long into. In this place of to resist the real you that you are to be heard as to speak, you will feel the insecurity of the physical body that is to be the ruler of this that you allow yourself to think. One is to dispel all emotions that are attached to this 'not enough' or 'cannot' positioning that one has allowed her/ or himself to be hearing or thinking.

You are the conceptional being of
progression into an ever forward motion
shall we say to desire this ever knowing
of yours to become a place of yours to
experience. The concepts that are placed
upon one is this we are to see one to
speak of oneself as being the holder
of self into, is a place of constraint
and non-seeing of her/ or his ability
to believe in a far greater existence
that is you within. Many are to succumb
to this voice of weakness shall we say,
in a shyness or fear to speak, that is
to rule over all wanting' s and desires
to be forth coming to live into.

In these concepts or views of self to
be seen into, one is to feel a sense of
regret and disappointment to rise from
within to feel as a failure or not ready
to progress into this new becoming as it
is to appear to be known to you to be.

There are many that hold deeply within
themselves conversations or comments,
even judging looks of impatience or
unjust that they have been witnessed to
or seen as to a certain response to times
or previous intention to have begun.

It is of this that one is to have a kind
and gentle approach to the thoughts
or inward conversations that are to
be revealed to this physical form to
digest. It is not easy we say to have
already an opinion formed within ones
thoughts to be thinking of that can and
will lay so heavily into oneself to
feel so constricting and tight to be in
a spot to be absolutely destroying to
this one that is wanting to believe in
himself or herself so desperately.

You are of this great this you are to know
and it is only you that can seize these
words or capture these comments that we
have spoken to let them rest within you
in a sense of self to be pleased to hear
of all that is to be spoken by your souls
voice, your voice of love, the words
of god that we be, you are to become
the chooser of the speaking's that you
hear to call of them what you wish.

One's presumable views {old views/
beliefs} of this that one is, is to be
a heaviness or a disability it appears
to this in human form to carry. For no
one sees of this that you hold into to

think as yours. It is a position of unjust that one thinks regarding this that she/he cannot do, have or become.

It appears limiting, does it not?

YES, we offer this to comment that in one's personality it is to be a fuse that refuses to light, no matter the encouragement or words of kind that are received, for if you are in this way to think of self as to not; then you certainly shall NOT. It is only of the personality being the holder of this intention within to be not in a sensing of to be worthy within this form of self to be that is to be the big stopper or holder back that they are seeing themselves to be. You are in many we see to offer, to perceive yourself as not able or lacking in ability to feel this pull or gentle guiding from within to be a request to step up or forward shall we say to let yourself succumb to these feelings of great desires, dreams and even goals to plan or to feel as though you are capable.

You are just in all that you be, you are exactly this in all your entirety to be.

It is decidedly hard to be in a place to be accepting, is it not?

> If in your voice to speak and your human brain to think this, than that is correct.

You are your own desirer within and if it is of the speaker or thinker to think that these desires, dreams or goals are not worthy of you to become than it is certain that you will not.

We speak in bold here to be spoken that many of you are holders of misread stories, old truths and conversations and circumstance to be spoken of in your voice to hear or from others that you have been or done certain things that are not to have felt as great achievements or attained your goals or never accomplished any greatness to be.

Your words, as we have spoken in many times to you to hear that these words of yours to speak are deadly to one's nature to be allowing of herself/ or himself to be bold, to be confident. For it is in these words that you speak to hear, that you are to face defeat, dread, anxiety, fear even as to what it is that you can and will be capable to let yourself even imagine to become a conceivable idea within.

Damaging these words, thoughts, and impressions are to lay, and they are to present to you in all your wrongness to be seen, thus in turn eliminates all your rightness and perfection in your very so choosing of this self to become that you lay defeated and deflated to the real words of truth that are to lay within just waiting to be allowed to be heard in a confidence by you. For in so many of you we are to witness this time and time again this valuable lesson that many are trying to learn, to experience, to shed of its holdings within to expand into another that will not, this lesson is to be grand within self, to be proud, to be heard, to be really just you.

You are not a place to sit into to judge. In this judgement whether of another or of yourself or to be thought of as to being judged, you are to discredit all that is absolute in all its righteousness within you. This very soulness that you are to be ever contained into you will distinguish her voice to be squelched within over and over again until one day in your deciding you are ready to shine and to shed this outer skin of unjust that you are to place upon oneself in this life and maybe the next and the next for you are the holder of ones soul experiences to learn, to fulfill.

So, you see you will know in all that is right within the time of your real unveiling to be accepted by you as this exact moment of your so NOW to be living into.

> You are right in all that you see to be,
> to do, for we and many have offered
> these words before in all that you
> do, see and be, you certainly are.

How does one begin; To see how great they are? It feels impossible from where I AM.

In one self to know, they are. Is this not, correct?

Many conversations have been opened into this space of which it is to be receiving of this certain knowing within this self to be great. You are the seer of all that you are, so would you not let yourself to always be the seer of GREAT. It is only in ones forming of thoughts to be held onto that they do not see great within. Why are you to compare yourself to another? for they are to not matter to us when we are assuming you, neither should they be of a matter to you?

You are the extraordinary light that is to beacon so brightly to the heavens and beyond of your forthcoming into this very essence of self to be. You were the decider of lessons to be felt and lived into, you were to ask of this growth & expansion to become yours to experience, you are the holder of this opportunity to be seen in all possibilities of this that you are. Let this be spoken of by us to you that we see only of a oneness in this very now that you are to see, this is your stance within that you must take to be accepting of all that you are and all that you are not. For in every are and not that is felt or uttered is a valuable lesson to be learnt, to grow, to expand, to cherish for of this it is that you will see only this that you are asking to speak to see and in this is your very own opportunity to take hold of this that you see being able to rise to be received as your obligation from within to be this person, to be this characteristic, to be this personality. For it was you who chose so decidedly here in this that we be to be you to feel as yours to understand. So, stand proudly into this place to receive of all that you may be attentive to see, and you will begin to remember to ask to know that this is you, the real you. Be kind in all aspects of self to be, forgive yourself if to feel weak within to change, be gentle here to self to see, for you are an adventurer of this planet in this unique way to be, so let yourself feel settled/ or gratified if need be or to dream big, desire and plan for it all has the greatness attached in your very original asking of this soul to experience to expand. So, you see in every doing you are in some way to be explained, being guided to become this that you really wanted to be.

Please speak about Dreams, Desires & Goals.

Are they not of importance?

YES, in a complete recognition of these to be spoke of in this way, one would be asked to question this of themselves. Is the dream, goal, or desire in its becoming a reason attached to something that one would think will make or change the current situation to appear to one as more pleasing or more pleasurable?

If yes to answer, then we would ask to question this to self to know; Does this mean that you are unhappy in this moment of to ask, and survey and WHY?

Is it to respond to a sense of inadequacies within, or is it in viewing of another, is it dissatisfaction within self to be, is it to be better/ easier/ more exciting over there instead of here?

It is in this that we are to offer to you; know that you are the feeler of all that you are to ask within and if you are to feel as though you are not enough in this deciding moment than you will not or never shall be content, happy, joyous or felt to be.

One is to ask deeper or speak this is to be preferred: What if I AM to say WOW, look at me here in this NOW that I BE.

Why, is it that I feel like I am not enough or have enough? In the reality of all truths, it is just this, *'You are the offeror of all that you see'.*

To find inner peace or sense of worthiness, self-love, a steadiness within oneself to know that they are ENOUGH in all that they are to be this NOW. One must lose the comparison, the judgment, the self-analysis, the woe is me.

START to ask, HOW CAN I BE MORE ATTENTIVE, MORE RECEPTIVE, MORE WILLING, KINDER TO ME?

For these are all eliminators of unwanted reasoning's and suggestions that have been placed over time by you and others in offerings to be viewed as yours.

GOALS are aspirations to be more this we agree if held in the right context to be. For often it is to be spoken of a goal as an encourager to self to strive, to achieve or obtain a better position or sensing within oneself to be.

It is a motivator, IS IT NOT? Let all this be said that in ones self to be thought of as not enough than they will not feel the obtaining or completion of this goal to have done the job so to speak that one thought it would do. So, we offer this to say, let the word or use of the word as you would understand it to be, to be an accepting within self to be a determination of this self to see always to ask for more, only in a willingness to know that you are already all that you need. A goal as such is a decision within oneself is it not to be made or completed by a certain date, time, measurement. If this is the true case of the goal setting to be offered to self to be seen into, then it is to feel as though you are of a must to do to become. Let all inhibitions within this frame of mind be released here to hear of this that we say. All certainties of self are self-driven, by the speaker of you that you are to hold intently within in a complete understanding of this that she/he is to know of you in this perfect NOW that you sit as to be correct.

DREAMS & DESIRES, Envisionment & Aspirations to become or see yourself into are they not?

Be deliberate in your desires to be this that you are, for they are the interpreters of all that you are to hold yourself to accept these desires as a you that you are to be. For desires are your own originality to be showing, flowing freely through imagination to this that you see to speak confidently of.

Dreams are inspirations within self to be the holder of the you that you establish deeply from within to be a succeeding. Let us offer that you already are to view of these dreams as a reality for to daydream or envision of this self to be in a dream like state to witness the offering, you are free to feel and relish in this acceptance of this that you already are to see yourself as the holder of. Your ability to see yourself in this way as such to be willing to release resistance as to where it is that your thinking mind is and allowing. You are able & willing to step into a world of imagination and a clear place of no limitations or boundaries, for to dream big is a saying so often heard to be expressed by those of you that do.

There is no resistance in here attached to this form to speak, for you have nothing to lose shall we say when you are willing to sit into this place with no limits, such as a goal or completion of to be achieved, so to dream and desire of it is a certain acceptance by you to be not held in a constraining way as to be completed in such time as to feel obliged or committed to.

WE SAY DREAM BIG. LET YOUR IMAGINATION ROAM.

We see of this to be somewhat of an asking to be accepted by most to allow of self to dream to envision or to float freely into. Here one has no limits, no disappointments, and your imagination is yours to be, no interpretations by others is needed, no explanations, no guidelines or how to guides or timelines. A sense of freedom within is achieved by allowing of self to be deliberately out of one's head to think to just be, freeing oneself of all constrictions as to think of this in a certain way is to be this, just this that you are to imagine yourself to be.

No one needs to know or hear you to speak of participation or a yearning to be a part of an accomplishment. They just are not. Feel as you are to willingly let yourself slip into a state of deliberate daydream and drift off into a total-ness of inner surrender to be accepting and succumbing to the all that is to flow.

Be present into this NOW, this moment of exactness as it is and you will always be present within this self to be ever hearing, ever seeing, always feeling and in a complete knowing of this that you truly are.

> Watch as these words of yours are to appear, ever present they will be for you to see as yours that were written by you this one in her/his NOW to feel from within the desires, dreams, and ideas that one in this space to reveal is to be the receiver of all that the true believer within has been asking for you to see, to feel, to remember into all this that you are to ask to become. They are maybe small or extravagant this is not to be of concern for all that ask are heard if to be spoken of in trust, faith and a heart that sits of open love. These words you write are hard for some it appears and this we know that these are the ones that are to be the real seers of the great that they be for to hold this within in a silence that has not yet been offered up to be heard will feel of the greatest intent to

be realised from within as ones deepest
desires to be revealed to be spoke.

Use this moment of opportunity to just
flow free, to express from this that you
know. You are the writer of all that is to
exist from within in the greater sensing
of this self to be. Feel not to hesitate
for to pause to think is to ask the human
that you be to step in to understand, the
less that human thoughts are suggested as
to be a guide into of what it is that one
is to realise, the freer you will become.

Let all that one's heart must speak, pour out. Let it be recognised as yours, in all your realness to be simply this. "JUST and CORRECT" in all that is spoken as YOU.

CHAPTER 5

SEEING ME

In ones realising of this true self
to see they will see the ……

'Beautiful you within ME'.

You are of this to ask are you not?

What is it that I AM to see in ME?

In ones boldness to be spoken of in this way, one must be always in a place to ask to see the real ME.

To be ever the willing witness to all that one is to willingly be present with their thoughts or suggestions as to the real ME being yourself to assume as the greater understanding of this that you BE.

You are the one, the only, the ever present, the ALL that is known as the creator to be present within performing in all of his or her capabilities the diligence within to be ever the speaker of righteousness to be heard swell from within to be spoken as this that you BE.

YOU are right to know that this is you that you are to see, in the allowing of oneself to see the real ME that you are where one is to begin, and for most it is to be a long arduous journey shall we say with much self-discovery attached to be witness to. The beginnings are often filled with a hesitation to start for the unveiling or unwrapping is often a hard task to bear. It is to leave one feeling naked and raw, torn emotionally, physically, and spiritually we will offer. The seeing of this self in this space of what appears to be vastly different to the one that she thought herself to be feels threatening and filled with dread it appears to most to offer. For to want to be in this place of total reveal in the first place begins as a simple question to ask,

THERE HAS TO BE MORE, DOES THERE NOT?

We speak these words often and repeatedly it seems to those of you that are to ask, for it is to be said that not all that embark upon this journey of spiritual reveal are to think of it to be as hard as others are to have expressed it to be. Many if not most will discover their road to travel to say in their most suitable way, the way to express self-thoughts associated with self-worth, self-expression, to find ones voice, or simply to feel better within is always to be a challenge to the one that is to look the deepest within, for it is of many that start that we see give-up or feel like they cannot comprehend this part of them that is to be revealed in essence of such a pureness that is to be discovered as this that they thought themselves to be not. Much learning is undertaken and many conversations of transgression within to be held here by self so denying of this self to speak at first, for here it is that it lays the difficult part that it will not simply just go away. The more you try to ignore the opening that is happening within, the harder it appears that one has to fight to let all this go and just try and resist the intention that it becomes from within to be heard. This is you we say, the greater component of all that we be to be speaking in your words of truth offering this to you to say....

THIS IS YOUR TIME.
I HOPE YOU ARE READY.

It is of this to say that like a can of worms to be opened it will not stop, first it is intrigue, then curiosity to be felt, studying of all that is to be allowed to be spoke will entice you even deeper within, research and contemplation into all that is to become a part of you to be heard will be reviewed and asked many questions and answers to be heard. You will dive deeper even still into this one that was once you, but feels to be different in every way, changing in moments of self to be this that appears to be a new you wanting to be revealed.

You will feel like another and in this we mean not to be yourself, for much integration has started to be yours to feel in the challenges of self to be found that are to be appearing to be seen in all this that you be. You start to doubt that this is what it was that you wanted, for nothing appears to make sense anymore. Does it not?

You feel lonely and this is where one is to begin her/his journey of the greatest being to ever know starts to emerge in all her truths, all his honesty's, in all her undeniable speaking's, in all his extravagance for you searched to find this to be heard and in here it is that they are to appear.

Your connection becomes strong in this you are to see yourself to grow and expand needing less to know from external realms to hear, but in more to become of a trust within that no one can come close to compare.   In trust we have spoken in many times of speech to be held by yours as to understand, for you are of this trust that maybe you just might begin to feel as a certainty that is to grow from within in an expansion to be known as the greater soul that exists deeper within this physical cast of form to be. You are so loved and in this you are to hear, YES this is the seeing of the real ME starting to appear.

LET THE ADVENTURE BEGIN, YOU ARE TO HEAR.

To view of this that you are is to be seen in a willingness to know that you are the adventurer that has embarked upon this glorious journey of expansion and growth.

It was of you, the seeker to ask to the all that be this great to be found in the all that you see. In one's place of which it appears to you to be standing, you are to be the real you that you are to see. It is of ones voice that spoke so strong in a definite of all that she was to become, to be willing to see this that she is to see as the real me that I AM.

IN this we ask you not to falter in your thoughts as NOT, for you asked decidedly so in your concept of this to be you, to experience in everything that you are to see in this reality of this self to be. You are the adventurer as one would call of self to be, know this that not all adventures are to be to travel afar, or even to say joyous in every way.

For the many of you the smallest of reveals are to be the greatest of steps to become in this ever-asking self of this that you are to be. You are in this one state of which it is to comprehend this that you are to know that you are to see you as the real ME.

What does it feel like to be the REAL ME?

I do not feel to know.

In this we feel the many of you to ask, for it appears to us to offer that so many of you are to feel lost and non-comprehending of the reality of this that you are to exist into. It is in this aspect of self to be not, that the many of you are to feel like you are not to belong or feel to progress, it is this heaviness that is to linger from within in ones understanding of this self to be. You are to evict these thoughts of this to be a wanting from within for you are the all that you are ever intended to be in this exact moment of which it is to appear to you to ask. This is your now! the most important stage of this life to be lived into and for now it is this that you are to see. Know this that in the very next now of yours to be you will be of a difference to be, you are the ever presenter of the all that you see to witness, so let your view change to contain the wisdom from within that is to explain.

You are love and loved in all that you think this self to be, let down your guards of disbelief for you are willing in this we say, to speak you are of us In every god like oneness to present.{ if in asking to speak of this one as god please choose of it to be yours}. Our oneness is held within all that IS. You are of him, you are his nature, you are his love, you are his understanding, you are his discipline, you are his heart, you are his filling to be felt, you are his touch in your all that he be included in you to be.

We sense of you here in a softened state to observe into the all that you have heard for this journey it appears has to start somewhere and if not here, then where.

If one is to continue to hold these thoughts as hard to resist than that is to be spoken of as your choosing in this moment of this that you BE. We are deliberate in the all that we speak there is much that is needed to be offered so little by little it is to be revealed to those of you that are to feel as just to begin. In trust it is that we speak to offer to you all that you need to be hearing to feel complete, let this journey from within unfold in all its honesty of its reveal to be yours, in only yours to allow. One must be resistant it is to be spoke to the most that are to offer up to you a not to know of this that you speak, let yourself grow here in this space of wisdom to be found for this is your wisdom unique in its wise to be yours to cherish as your own.

Many will try to sway you from your post, this we have been observing for as long as IS to be just, we are ever present in this all that is to be found and if it is of you to find that it does not feel to suit you to think of this that one must. Then please do not.

WE ask of you to continue upon this human journey, {soul filled it is that you are to know unwillingly yet for some}, that you are to become, and you will in your time be a willingness to feel this that we are to sit into ones heart to unfold, to open wide in the all that you be to ask of this, we are real in every essence that is. So, let your self be wise to your thoughts to think of us as not, it is in only ones time to be that we will be felt ever present within once again.

BEING ME....

It is here that I am to feel as though I am to begin.

Dear One, let us offer to you straight up, to begin is to have already existed into this very understanding that we are so of. For it was of your asking in a willingness, your decisive deciding and deliberate intent to be. So, of this that you are here in this very place in which it appears that you are to ask to begin. You began many moons ago shall we say, for much has been already lived into and formed or decided into as to this very reasoning of such to arise from within this that you be to see yourself into as to ask or feel in this that you think of yourself to need to begin. All that you have surveyed or undertaken was deliberate intention to be called your own souls calling of the greatest of intent from within to grow, expand and learn, to make your way home again. So, cherish this very essence that you see yourself allowing of this need to begin to rise once again. It feels new in every newly discovered concept that you are to undertake, for you are in the midst of the most ever continual aspect of self to view, to be the next continuation of this uniqueness that you are to encourage from within ones certainty to have asked to establish so devotedly into this being of love that you are to ask to witness its rising as to feel as though you are ready to begin again.

Seeing oneself as a progressive intuition within self to be, one is deliberate in all forward movement to be progression, is one not?

For it appears to us upon this planet that you all so divinely live into, you are to be non-responsive in ones attitude to the need to be of more than what it is that you are.

So, to feel as though to begin entitles oneself a feeling or sensing of to wipe away the dreaded or the regretted and to let all fall away to make way for the unfolding or revealing of a new self to step into this place of which to start again.

Can we offer here to speak into, that you are always ever changing. Never to be in what it was that you were, for all NOWS are changing and certainly can be different from the last. In ones willingness to see only of this NOW that we speak as your entering into an exactness that you be in this very NOW that you so see, one will feel of the difference if they are being responsive to the very being of existence that is of you so divinely lit from within this that we be to be the shower of you to see this that you truly are.

We see it of this to offer; that in one's deliberate intent to negate of all that one is to have become in this very presence that you are to present to us here, you are in all reality this that you desired to be. You have treated yourself to this very experience not for the human component to live, love or be {although on first thought or presentation of it, it may appear this way} but purely for the souls component that you are to have asked to experience as this amazing journey that shall be ever unfolding in all certainty if you are to be the willing receiver in all her truths to be heard from within as she is guided and gifted in the most extraordinary ways if one is willing to be open from within to the ever speaking voice of truth to be yours to listen into as this great asking as yours to simply just be.

For you are all in this very beginning of self to find one decidedly so and in this so seeing of one to be placed into this position of which it is to appear as to begin. {Let us offer that it is in this human form that you are, that you are to awaken shall we say to words been offered to describe of what this feeling is to be explained as by many}. It is in here that you become decidedly insistent to this inner knowing to be revealed that there is more, it is okay to ask, and you are to want to know of this that is for the likelihood that you are to be hooked seems impossible right? GUESS AGAIN!

It is a natural progression within this humanoid that you are to be accepted as that you will feel the emotions of self-worth to grow and to embrace this want to expand or gain greater knowledge into this new way of which it is that one is to speak to hear to be that entices the older viewing of you to become a relic shall we say in an eagerness by you to dump this heavy exterior to become of a lighter, more accepting, eager to love, decidedly you to be seen into that we are to feel as your response to this that we are to be ever contained within you to be accepted as a new way into which it is that you shall look to begin.

So, are you offering that the 'I' that I AM NOW is the new me?

You are always the new 'ME', for to expect anything else other than a new you into every available moment of your so now to be described as a transition into this new that you be is to be non-accepting of change to be yours to be of.

One is always to be a new ME, for this is the truth that exists so deeply embedded within to be always forth coming ever to evolve to be more, existence in a want to become fulfilled and learnt of all the ways in which it is that one was to ask to discover so accept this as your answer to be YES! this is the newer you that you are to be, NOW, NOW and NOW.

See yourself as an ever-changing version of you for no two now's are ever the same. So in this essence that you really are, you are just an interpretation in this given instance to be seen into to be of this that you see to know, so change your thoughts, change your view, change your words, change your view, change your impression of self to be, change your view, you are a decider of change to transition if allowing of this to be performed in such a confidence that you hold intuitively within, only if in an asking to always be more.

I STAND IN THIS WILLINGNESS TO SEE ME.

It is here that I view of myself as ME, becoming of this that I Am to be. My interpretation of ME may be different to the way it is that you view ME. This I say is okay, let this be your way to view ME, but know that this ME that you think you see is not really ME. I am always to know this ME as to be nothing like the ME that you think that is ME. For my image that I project is this that I feel as the ME for YOU to see. The real ME, 'I' will change my thoughts upon of how it is that I look to you, for you are to see ME as the ME that you are needing to see for you. Let all that I appear to be seen by ME is to be just for ME. I look lovingly upon this reflection that I see, and I am glad that it is ME in all entireties reflected out to ME. I AM willing in this now to look even longer at ME to see this that I see. This is ME, the real ME that I have longed to see. Deliberately I face into ME to view this that is the YOU I see. The YOU that YOU are that sits into my heart, the YOU that YOU are that challenges me to become MORE of this that

> I AM, the YOU that YOU are to be ever
> present within ME guiding, offering,
> and calling to ME to be more of this
> real ME that I now wish to see. This ME
> is the YOU that YOU are to ME to see.
> I now see YOU reflected in ME to see.
> YOU are ME. I AM YOU.

In this observation of this that I am to stand here to see as my representation of this that I BE.

I ask deeply into myself, is it this that I AM to be.

AM, I seeing the true ME?

Ever asked of yourself this to know?

In one's observation of all this that she has become is the reasoning behind the voice or thoughts of this to ask of self to be seen in truth to be this that one is.

Many suggestions and concepts of thoughts have been offered to one to think into as this to be this that is represented here into this NOW that is the chosen moment to be seen into as this you.

Are you this you we hear you say, YES, is the deliberate response to all that are asking for you are the receiver of the all that you are to be responsive to and in this regard, you are exact in this exactness to be this that you see. For many that have asked to become, you already are, and it is this that you see that you are. We offer here in these words to speak to flow that you are the seer of all that you have obtained and strived to become to be in this very exactness into this that you appear to be. One in her/his willingness to experience or to gravitate into or towards is the place of true desiring of this innerness to ask to experience, and it is upon this path of which you be presently placed that you are to be seeing into this that is represented in all of the trueness that you are to be. For you see in your physical eyes it has been or maybe still is a place of unworthiness, disheartenments or disappointment perhaps that the many of you are to feel into, this we say eliminate these external thoughts as such to be forced upon one to think into as to be this in a physical sensing of this self to be, for yes you are physical in all that you think to be but you are far greater in revelation of this self to be allowing of one to think into. For in this unseen part of you that is to be made apparent in this now to be witnessed into as a you to be seen as just an interpretation of all that you are to carry to think into as you, you will feel this deliberateness to rise from within you to want of to see into a different perception of this self to be. A different view to be a wanting to be placed into your thoughts as this that you are to be more, to be ever efficient into the capabilities that lay within to change your minds thoughts to be more trusting of your mind's eye to see yourself as a dominate decider from within to be partaking into a particular understanding to transgress further inward to become ever more magnificent in her calling of this to be known as you to be the real you to see.

I hear myself speak.

It is of how this one is to view of herself/ himself to be seen into as how this story is to be told....

Look deeply in a space of contemplation where you feel all truths are to be always told to be heard. For it is in these honest truths to be spoken that you will feel the you that you think or thought of yourself to be rallying from within in a wanting to stay this way that you have always been to see.

Let yourself stand against this resistance so strong and determined it would appear to be in a gracious heart to be spoken of all that will be and is revealed. Think not to second guess or to apply a judgement of words or thoughts to be spoken of all that is to appear, for this unveiling within is to be the most revealing, trying yet honest sittings that you have sat into to become. Many opportunities are offered to grow upon this planet to be yours to feel contrast and difference to be felt as yours to partake into. Release this deliberate attempt to be just this in a solidness or seriousness that you feel you must stay in tuned within to for you are in all allowances to be accepted as yours to see to feel in this space of love. Be sensing to feel this determination to grow from within to feel as this REAL ME, this 'I' that you be in total-ness of this that we BE, watch in a sensing of the real you to unfold for she/ he surely will in this place of recognition to be held and heard so deeply and divinely within. This we say is to have been offered by many that have offered this to repeat, it will rattle your existence, it will speak in words of not yet heard, it will become of you to want to feel this change to wash over you to know that you are this magnificence that you speak to hear and in this very glimpse it would appear to be a very different you to be peering back out at YOU.

IN this space of LOVE, I chose to sit

Blessed be this space that one has chosen to sit, for it is in this space that one allows for all of time to be stopped, all thoughts to be just this that they are, all others are to be ignored or in a deliberate attempt to be not seen for they will slowly disappear into this space that you once were thinking to have feared. Feel as you are to relax even more, you find your breath to sound as though it is almost out of sink to this old rhythm that it once was to breathe to. A new rhythm from within this physical form is to take over in a sense to say that you will soon start to feel this graciousness appear in every way, you stop now to feel your breathe in all that you see, the ease into which one becomes in alignment with all that they are to see is a new experience, yet one that is gladly received. You wait for the old to revisit or re-enter the scene again, she does not, you will not need her to return. YOU start to see yourself in a completely different way, for why is it of this YOU to see that you have not noticed her there before in this that you have looked.

Thoughts of compassion, tenderness and love are to overtake the all that you sense to be in a place of freedom yet to be, you must we say let them be of this way for they will too find this to be in their own way. You easily release things that once were to be a heaviness to be spoke, you sense this willingness within to be spoken, you hear your words change to a kinder voice to speak, you are patient with this learning new, you stand taller in this confidence to have been found, you sense this to be you in the all that you see, you are of this love you are to know, and it becomes deliberate within this REAL YOU to see. For suddenly it becomes apparent that this is the REAL YOU that you are to have been seeing, it was just that she/he was covered over in a sense by the many that have spoken of you to see and of your own words of entitlement as not to be, you see in the new view that you are to ask for to be is where you have been all along, hiding in the shadows of the self that was not ME. This self you feel stepping out of the dark to be seen in all her light is to be the REAL YOU that you so deeply yearned to know.

Authors thoughts on being ME...

[My unveiling from within this that I be]

It is quite a revelation to be received from within or let's say the eternalness that is you, when one is to sit to adjust all thoughts and oppressions of this that she thought of herself to truly be. When the certain feeling and of this you will know of which feeling it is to be. For, I dare say it is the one that got you here. Ones sensing of the questions that are to rise from within, in a nagging insistence to be felt, to be heard, to be dealt with. For you see it was this that stirred me from within, a certain wanting to begin to ask am I seeing the real ME.

IS THIS THE REAL ME THAT I, SEE?

Over time and circumstance of which there have been many I shall say that I have let another be my response or sight of this that I should BE.

Why is it I asked often, was I not willing to be ME?

To this I accepted my innerness in all her gracious heart to offer, through spirited conversations and tears of non-recognition, then recognition into this thinking that this is not to be me, I allowed for myself and of this I still do, to be a honourable listener to my higher self, {you may call of it in difference to me this I say is your own correct way, whether it be gods voice, spirit or righteous love it all is spoken the same}.

So, in this higher self's voice to speak I heard words that were to open my heart in a trust to be received to be of this wanting to get to know ME. I dropped all pretence of what it was that I THOUGHT that others thought. There I said it, this is exactly the truth to be heard by myself and you in this place that we meet. It was all in my thinking of what I THOUGHT that others were thinking that I got lost so to speak. For it did not matter my higher self-revealed of what it was that I thought in another's thoughts of me to be, the truth lay easily to see.

>It is of what I thought of ME,
>that was letting me down.

I realised after a while listening to this voice of LOVE {and trust this when I say that you will find yours in your own special rhythm to speak, this you will}. So, I stopped every now and again to experience this voice in her rawness and honesty to reveal to ME exactly of what it was that I was like. It was I will say like getting to know a stranger that I thought I might have liked. She {my higher self} encouraged ME to blossom and bloom and let me say I still have a lot of this to do. For you see this I have learnt, and I am to know that this is okay that some days it is hard to cherish this voice that I know is correct and right to speak in all her might for me to hear as correct in the days that one is to feel of doom and gloom, that we all face in this physical form.

But let me speak here in this voice that I have found to be mine that I love in this real ME that I see. I asked to sit into this space to hear, and to be taught by revealing's from within of all learnings from her to be spoke.

This higher self-spoke in all truths that she was and in this you to will find out that all if not most are willing to step out of the shadows that we feel as not allowing of this that we BE. For you see they are in all Ernst of your true self to be, trying to be seen, willingly you, showing you how to shine your light upon this that you are to see yourself as

'SIMPLY THIS REAL YOU TO BE' .

YOU are the real YOU that you aspire to be, she has not never been in all that you have tried to see, to be. You already were in the becoming of this....

CHAPTER 6

"BEAUTIFUL YOU THAT YOU ARE WITHIN ME".

IN HERE WE SPEAK

To be deliberate within oneself to recognise all that appears to be unfolding as to be seen in this new way is of you this that we say. You are presence to be felt as this of us to be, for you are the exactness in this deciding that you have chosen to become. We see all of you in this bright light to beam for you are the true adventurers, the true journeyers, the true seers to see and to be of this composition of this humanoid to be. You are the receiver of all that you intended, and it is to be partaking into this exact moment of thought to be that you are, it is not of chance or circumstance it is of choice by you to have been deliberate into your asking of this to be discovered or revealed to you in this very essence to be called your time. You are the receivers of all that is to unfold and in ones directness to become into this that you so chose. You, as many will feel often at times to be exposed to many situations and circumstances that you do not feel relating to or rather to be in disbelief to think of these as to have chosen. Yes we offer here this is hard to comprehend for the many that are to just feel their search as to begin one will find these words of choice to be heard as a misunderstanding at first to be thought of as correct, let us further you here to a time when you will accept of all that you hear spoken in love by you and your forthcoming of self to be divinely reintroduced shall we say to the figure or human that has got in the way. She/he is gently in standby mode shall we say at your disposal in every possible way for it is of us that you are to know as this great that you be and in all that you know. For it has not been this particular human form, but the real spark of you who is to have been the carrier, the seer, the requester, the knower, the desirer to become all of these intuitions and truths to be known in this space of which it appears you will slowly start to comprehend, for you will find your greatest discovery is of the you that lays inside, or so it is to feel as first for of this it is that many are to speak but to really feel this truth to be told it is of all that be both seen and unseen that we are that are you to become or to know that you have already been. It is in this defining moment that is to reveal or open for you shall we say that ones expectations of us are to feel as though they are to get in the way. It is in the way that this human is to think in variance to us to be exact and right and yet you to be fraught and concerned into the all that you are to imagine of us to be. We are simply this as it is to appear no introductions or titles to be worn, for we are the explicitness that is all of this to be always and forever in its entirety of which it is to BE.

It is in these words of love and just that we are to offer this message of complete pure blessed love. For we are the overseers or the one to be presented here in all that you are to hear, we cherish this time to be spent with you all in thought and to feel of your righteousness that is to be exposed here to be heard as these words that are to contain a vision of self to be loved in an understanding of all that are to pass your way are to be purposely poised and put directly into your path for you to know. There are many here that in which it is that we speak that you have designed and interpreted as yours to know and you will find your journey to be complete in an understanding of how it all shall go. Hand over the keys lets offer it this way, for you are just the vehicle that is being driven by the innate driver within, she is in charge of all that you so desire of this to be. You have written your life's map, and in such intrigue, it was of you this lightness within that held close contact to the believer of this that you all will be. So, let yourself hand those keys willingly to the universe, the god, the love, the voice of truth whoever it is that you need to speak as the one for you, for it is in this letting that one is to give, to step forward out of the shadows shall we say that you have stood in to feel and find your way.

There is much to be previewed YES, we offer you this as to be correct, but in ones directness to become bold in her way she will feel of this intent rise from within to become an internal calling for all that we be to correspond into to be believed. It is of us that we are to speak, that we are completely of you in all this entirety of this that you be, solid and focused only on {in} love to feel like you are derived of this to know as you in this moment of which it is that we are to speak. Know this as yours to grasp, this understanding of this that we be. This you will in your entirety of the all to be revealed upon your return to the great and beyond for that is ultimately why you have decided to come along, to experience this life once again, to cherish this life of duality it would seem, to live into a world that is ever ready to expand, to experience this transition that is at hand for you are the greatest leaders in this unveiling or newness to become. It is of you dear ones that we are to see. It is you that are the light bearers, the holders of this love to be so bold and to grow into this expectance that this is of what love should be. To feel in your originality that this is yours to belong for you are simply placed here in ones eagerness to begin another interpretation of this form to be cherished to witness oneself in all aspects that are to be previewed.

For you have travelled far and wide it is to appear from within this that you speak to us to know, and it is in this journey how ever it is to feel that you, the real you, the greater you, the soul within this that you be is to be the boldest speaker of this that you be she/ he has guided you here to interpret this lesson or teachings or beliefs once again to understand. For all that are here sharing this Earth with you are to begin yet another phase shall we say of this unique experience of humanism to be betrayed as one of the greatest attempts to evolve, to expand, to love and to feel into this incredibly unique beautiful world. So, let us say you are never alone or separate to us for this is incorrect in all that we are just. You are the boldest of wisdom to be held and in ones forgiveness of this that they are to see as not correct or right they will feel this heart space to open and feel light in here as it is that we are first to be felt for our sensing of you is this unique voice of love to be first found for the one true commander of this all that you be.

Standing deliberate in all aspects of him or herself to see. You are the wanter of all this, so let yourself feel this release from the struggle that you have been dedicating your life to, so that you may step out of the darkness so to speak that has been holding you back, let the sun shine upon your face and feel the energy that you are to begin to unwrap this newest aspect of you, for you are all faceted with this unique skin to be felt as an entrapment to self or this earth to see yourself in. Know this that you are, just the carrier of something so bold and golden in all the light that she/he be, and you will feel of this human body to give way to become a knower and asker into the all that BE.

We are forsaken in the many that feel as though not to ask, for to ask feels like they must. Does it not? You must never be or do of anything that you will not feel to be right, it is in this great knowing of this that we are that all that speak are heard in a truth to be unique.

It is your expression from within that we truly see so leave all residue behind of the human that you be, strip off the outer layers of have to and cannot, be bared to the brilliantness that you see in us to be you in every ray, aspect, and conversion to be. You are to be brilliant in all that you command. You are of this that is of nothing this you are to know. You are to be the deliberate creators of most and more to always be, for your growth is dependent on your intention to be. It is of us here in which it is that one is to think of us to speak, but let the truth be told that this is your voice of love, your messages of great, your completeness within that is yours to evoke for you are all this incredible being of light and love to always be.

So, shine your new shine and let the light fully in. For you are to become a reflection to this self to see always the,

'Illuminate being of love & light to shine'

"Beautiful you that you are within ME"

It is of us that we are to speak, one voice of many that are bold in the sensing of them to be. We are all in this entirety to be spoken of in this way to be heard by the many that have decided to turn to face of us again. You are all deliberate creators of self to be, so hear this as your truth. You will find of us again, for you are never lost or neglected to be this that you see. This is only just the beginning for some to think of it in this way, let that be correct for you upon your journey and along this way of life to be felt upon this planet as such to be your earth, to explain ~ you are craving an intention from within to become of us again.

It will always be your connection home and do not despair for you will not ever lose your way or forget your way, it is of us that are to guide you through these veils of eternity that are to be felt as to be unseeable to most. But know that upon your bed of life to end that you will see the light of magnificence to be seen as your tunnel or passage of your return to be, fear not of these words to end our speech with for it is spoken of with love and a completeness to be heard that this is us and in your turn you will find yourself to be absolute complete and to love of this that you have partaken into this life to have been.

For it is this journey that you are upon that one must cherish as his or her own, for it is not of another that you must delve into to see for it is only this reflection of you that we are to see.

You standing there so right and true in this absolute placement of this here to be your now. So, open up your channels of wisdom and your voices of love to be let to flow through to you like a river that is to never stop, and you will feel of this intention that you so decidedly chose to become as the greatest gift that one is to have received in your innerness to know of you to be.

Believe in this uniqueness that is you, for you are never to be repeated again in all of time that is to be far and beyond of what you can or will ever comprehend and to know of this that you are now is in this perfect placement to be seen as you, this very you that you are to be seen in here by us to be real. We are of you this very essence to be found upon ones willingness and response to be the asker of all to be heard, you will all find this feeling within to be yours to return to the one true belief that you are and this we say in the most loving way is you, this is the love that all have come to speak of to know.

For this is your journey of self to become in all honesty of yours to feel, this is LOVE that we are to wish to be told in all that are to speak of us as in this bold way, for in our greatness to be is the very essence of you to be.

We are silent to some, and this is okay, for they will hear of us in their right way whether it be this now of which it is to appear as this one to be or another that is to be presented again to be felt as a different now to be present. For now of this that you are ever in your now of which it is to begin and in ones sensing of this to be spoke know that you are never the same as the one that is to appear here to be hearing of this that we speak, for many infoldings are to become and in ones letting of self to know of this to be the dear ones that we are to be ever present within and to surround you from afar you will all interpret this life in your own way for that is of what you have written to become your guide to be speaking to you about. She has seen you in many travels so far and is of the truest intention to know of you to be thus far so let her hold your hand and walk with you this far for this life is only one of many to have been and to have become and in this one to have thought to forgot you will cherish all that you have received too learn upon your return. We see the many of you to feel as though there is a change in the air shall we say and to feel of this now is a certainty that you described as it to be yours to partake into upon this life upon this to be. You all saw of the great adventure to begin to become so you rallied within self to be shown of this one and let this be known that you were all the greatest of essence to see in self to know that you were to be sustained by this planet you know of as earth and that you were to inhabit her in this great that she be to experience and cherish a life such as thee. For so much has been undertaken by thee to experience to gain notches in your belt shall we say not all of good it would feel or to be spoke of in an earthly way, but to expand your soul that you be, to shine your light even brighter it was to feel of all this that is intended, was and already has, was your dreaming and desiring of this to be. For you are rich beyond your wildest dreams to be the holder of this so bold to be seen if only it was that one such as thee could see of this extraordinary being that you are to be seen into as us so that this it is that we must speak to you to know if only for you to listen in these words that we are to have spoken; *you are and always will be this evolving being of such extravagance to be.* So, hold on tight and let us revel in your light for it is of this journey that we came prepared in the all that you shall become to be the voice of truth that is to be heard by this one as you the deliberate creator of this self to be.

Relish and rejoice in this deliberateness that you bare for you are the one, the love, the truth, the gods voice to be spoke, you are the leader, the master, the seer, the internal wisdom of all of us here. Let us hear of your voice to be spoke. We watch of you all as you are to wake up realising and relinquishing into this very essence that you are to remember to be seeing of once again that you are way more than you could ever imagine of yourself to be seen into as a physical spokesperson of self to be. Feel this intent to rise from within finding her/ his way to the temple of love that you hold within, this is to be heard as your heart, the space from within that is grand and explicit in the decider of all that you are to be. Sing your song, let your voices be carried for you are all the soldiers of love shall we say that carry this eternity within to be ever spoken of in grace and faith to the all that are to be the listeners to hear that just maybe if you are all to speak in your voices that we love so dear, many others will hear even if just in a second to hear of you to speak and they too will feel this love that you are to beam to become and urgency from within to be felt to be understood as this that they have chosen to be their greatness to be lived here upon this planet to be.

> So, in our final words of this that we are to speak, know of us that you are so greatly loved and held in all absolute and complete that we be.
>
> For you are the children of god it is to say in this way of which it is that this one is to speak. For you are all the windows of this greater soul to be, the lights that shine from within us to be held so deep. Let your rays be seen by all that are to interpret this light as their own and they to ac will you, feel this connection to self to be made, and to know of this beautiful message as the all that is to be contained within and into the all that be seeing of this love as the utmost importance that everyone upon this planet is to be.
>
> It is just in this your NOW that we ask of you to BE, to see of this you and ME in the all that simply are to be ······

LOVE *in its entirety to be.*

CHAPTER 7

REALISING WITHIN

Know to feel of this that is spoken of as love, for we are all so intricately entwined within the ONE that be called in this name as to explain.

The entirety of self is complete in all formations of this that it is undertaking, to be perceived into and of this we are to be guided intuitive alliances into all that is to be felt to rise and reveal in this space of awakening as such that one is to feel the need to do. In ones naming of certain elements that are to be held within to think of this physical form as a holder of the sleeping giant shall we say and to be in a place of recognition once again to be feeling into this sensing of self to be the holder of this to be great. It is magical in this we say, for to feel your sense of worth to be more in actualness than a physical need to see of the pathway to success to be of this one in love to stand once more as you have come here to understand of this self to be a deliberate creator of all that be.

See of yourself in this place of rest to be relived into this sensing of this illuminate ability from within that is to open up all channels of this self to see, forgiving of all that was to be thought of as hard and unjust that one has listened to or held onto as this that they thought of themselves to be. For you are the eliminator of all that is to be seen into as wrong to know of the correction that lays within this voice that speaks so divinely for you in a correct and kind voice to speak. Feel as this voice is to become determined to be heard and to instil once again a sense of knowing in the all that you are. Many moments of hesitation have been yours to sit into of this we are sure, to witness as many along side of you have exclaimed to be right to say in every way. To feel this hesitation is a sensing that is felt within to be an asking of more to see, is it not? Feel yourself just to let go of the all that has held you to here is felt as a big release, is it not?

It is in ones reluctance within to be always asking as to bounce off another's opinion or to seek a solution from a friend or to study, read or find answers from the outer reality as it is to appear. Many are still to be seen in this position of which it is to ask for it has been a deliberate need that one has developed here in this life to be human to speak, that in ones opinion to be not all that is right and correct and to be seen in a different light by others and to hear of a voice that speaks only of love is to be the journey that many have decidedly taken upon.

What if I feel perfectly placed and have no desire to hear this voice, or to envision spirit, source, angels or guides of which you speak.

We hear this in many that are to speak that they appear to see others that are not this way inclined and appear to hold no information or words to speak about love, spirit, source or etherical beings at all. In one's placement here to be they are the choosers of all that they are to see. Look with intent at these ones that do not feel the need to speak in this language as such that you do, for often it is that ones are so in tuned within themselves that they are living their life perfectly formed and decidedly so in this aspect of themself to grow. It is not to say that they are not of spirit or source to be known for all that are, are in a sub conscious way deliberate asker of all that they ask and see it in an exact way as for it to appear. These are the ones that look to not be spiritual or evolving to be, but they are the ones that are to hold out their hands and the universe delivers, does it not?

This is correct to say, for some they have their formatting within to be exact, always acknowledging of more to come they believe in every entirety of this that they be to always be worthy of more, often to not suffer setbacks or unjust, they are to be the biggest fan to trust this self that they be and only know of what it is that they see to be all that they need. It appears to differ in many that you see for all are to experience their journeys as in an asking of it to be, so let all that appear to enter your scene to never be reminded by voice or to speak, for if it is of this subject that they do not speak or feel the need to be of, they will not hear your words of love or more importantly feel your heart to be. Many are to stand out alone it would look to appear to see of them obtaining all that they are asking of this life to be and in this we say that they have accomplished to see all that they are wanting for thee. They may not feel this intent as us within but know of this that we certainly are to be. All are to view of us in their own way whether it be fully in or just tipping the surface so to speak. Let all that becomes yours to know be just this and let others be, for those that are to see us in your way will certainly fall upon your path in no uncertain way, be ready we say for all that are to survey of you here into a belonging as such that is to become of you in every way will either feel of your heart as theirs or look to see a different way. This is okay and it is of this that we are to know that we are all to be loved and aligned in every way.

Perceptions of self are different in ALL, I see.

YES, this is correct to speak and in this it is that one is to hear, that all are the true perception of self to be seeing into, for all are to be a resounding from within this unique understanding that we are of to be. WE see many if not all capable and knowing of this that is to feel as to be an awakening begin. We are part of all journeys in every moment that they are to be presented in this way, so let all that are to pass or speak be entirely theirs to hear it as their truth to be.

Separation forsakes us, does it not?

In unity we are all. And of unison it is that we are to become again. It is often not felt like this to be told, many are determined it is to see that they are separate to many and are to eliminate or be ignorant to great love from their hearts to be felt as simply of ONE in all.

In this humanoid that you be hearing of all that is right in YOU, is a difficult task to speak of it in this way and to be a competitor to many it will be a long arduous task shall we say in the comparative way. In the sensing to know of self to be untied in this extravagant understanding of this that we all are of and the eternal realms of existence it is to follow your inner knowledge as it is to unfold, it always does in its own prescribed time.

It is in the great divide of the 'I' that causes rift and separation to have been a sensing of all that have re-entered to be found here once again, will feel of the ego at large to divide this that they are. To see of oneself in this egotistical way is yes, your thought of lessons to be taught but to preview of it in a human way will devour you to speak of as an innerness to keep. For to see yourselves as separate as the many of you do you are to lose this intuitive trust that you so divinely placed forever within to be this that you are of the one and all that are to expand. So, believe in this that we speak to offer here to your thoughts to access that you are the whole combined universes to see and if one is to alienate their potential to be receiving in most, than they will struggle to find this voice of love that speaks so lovingly. So, it will feel as though you are here as a separation to be experienced by you, we will never let you go. Trust in us when we offer, you are all so lovingly placed and a definite part of this that is the light, so feel no remorse in this to speak for you will all return to this that is to repeat to you ever knowingly so.

> YOU are complete and
> loved in all that you BE.

You speak of the universes complete within. Can you speak more on this?

The universe as one would see of it in your eyes to explain would be to hold all of you here. This is correct in a certain aspect to speak; the universe is a deliberate intent to have become for all of you there. In ones true sense of the word would it be not to have it explained as the ever knowing, ever growing aspect of self, for it is in this that you BE, the same in all regards of it to be seen.

You are of this unique matter that is to constantly change, entertain movement throughout and a deliberate knowing of all that is itself. It is in this sensing of self to be willing to hold of this to know that you are the exact same in existence of this that became. Deeply void of all that is to be not and to be the same for it is in this seeing of yourself to be thought that you are more than you have ever imagined. This universe that you speak of as raw and only partially discovered or encountered is to be the exactness that lays within, for the you that you are all to see is only to skim the surface of what it is that we see. We acknowledge of you all here in this element of self to see a physical sensing of this form to be but know this to be true that you are certainness to be eternity from within and you will escape this entrapment to be, thinking of this self in such a limiting way as to be only of what it is that you can see. Close your eyes we offer to all as an inner observation of this that you should do. You will let loose all constraints to be seen and if you are to just envision of the supreme then this is the truth that you shall see to begin as an endearment from within to be yours to see of this that we be. Encased in thoughts limited as such that you are only in what it is that you can touch will be deliberate to see in ones state of ecstasy that you are to be seen in the most that you cannot and will endeavour to find this voice of love that is to speak in all her truths of you to be. Here you will start to notice that in this that you see is only to just touch upon of what it is really, for to begin to explain goes way over the reality of most to picture themselves of intricate dust, loving in all that they be decidedly so to have become. In ones forming of this self to have been a interaction for learnings and mastery of this soul to be felt, it is of this one that is to be the founder of all that one is to see, and words to be spoke have never applied limits as to being or not, so find this space within oneself to be not to judge in what it is that one sees, look to the night skies and know that it is heaven that you are blessed to see in its most grandest way to ever be spoke and in here it is that you will find us.

The composition of All that be ever continuing to expand and grow we are limited by none in a sensing of all that we be. In us it is that we part in a transformation to become a deliberate being as such that is to partake into the very everything that you see and in the everything that you do not. This is us in our honesty to be spoke and you will feel of us first before you are to see.

Your universe is extravagant to most, is it not? Feel this to know that this universe that it be is to sit so in its entirety to be held within many universes to be of the ALL, the one and the eternity that they all shall be. Eager to progress in every which way, becoming of this that is to be the holder of all that is to become. So, it is in this that we say close your eyes, breathe it all in, for you are to see in this truly magnificent way that this is you in every way, a trillion universes and opportunities held within to become of this divine LOVE in it all simply again.

It is hard to imagine that something so big can be held within this that I be.

In ones thinking of self to be a holder as such is a human aspect within the logical mind to be a container of sorts. Yes, this is of what it is that we hear the many of you to speak but if only one could acknowledge this to say that they are more in every way, for to feel of self as to hold everything within is it not to offer to you to think of yourself as to be a deliberate intender to be this. So, let your thoughts of self to be an expression of freedom from within to be not in the need to hold us so close for in this it is that we will not. We are every-thing in presence to become, so in ones thoughts as to be needed to be within is limiting in this thinking mind to suggest. Let yourself feel of us to roam, flowing easily and never constrained nor held, it is not of us. We are the continual movement, expansion, and flow of all that you see and in all that you do not. We are the extravagance in the grand and also the minute` in most for it is of us to be explained in this way. Think of us to be free and effortless as a breeze billowing and blowing for this is of you to be thought in self to be resistant to none and resilient to most for if you are to encounter a storm shall we say you will bend and break if you are to hold to tight. So, let yourself be gentle and softened to bend, freedom to speak and of light to shine out of every shadow that appears from within for you are just as you appear. Look within your skies at night no defining boundaries to be kept or limitations to see. This is you and me in all that we be, entwined and gallivanting as one.

There is no you or me or them to see or speak just this that is,

ONE.

Universal Love as we offer, is this that is spoken of as thee. You are all equipped and so divinely fitted within this intention to be. In this love that we speak of grandeur and righteousness to be spoke, it is of this love that we evoke, a sensing from within the all that are to feel of it to rise in its own appeal to be sensed to be deliberate in this way that it is. You are all universal love to be explained, boundless, limitless, merging & entwining and ever continual into itself to become. You became out of love and you shall return to it in the same way. Benevolent beings of love with a heart to be spoken of by us in every way. You are the dreamers, the askers, the seers, the masters, the goddess's, and warriors all the same equivalent to this that you became.

Endearment it is for you to feel in all that is revealed, for you are the willingness that sat within us to choose this very being of soul to become to be extravagant in all that she/he is and was and will be to become. SO, let your universal love be one to shine so brightly to surround the all that you be, do and speak to let others know that you see in this of them to be the universal love that is to be found in all of humanity, existence, and planets to surround, for you are all evolved in this entirety to be, so let your universal love be allowing to run free.

CHAPTER 8

SURRENDER

{then surrender some more}

Hear of this as it is offered; In ones choosing to continue to fight no matter the losses that are to be felt or the gains to be made, this is allowing of the human component that is you to be felt as in turmoil from not only the external ravages that one perceives but more importantly of the innerness that is you that is in disregard of all this that you are choosing to see as a war to be won to succeed as to become of who or what.

The more beautiful, the wearer of the best, the bigger house, the loudest to speak, the better one, the one to offer more, the one that has more, the one that fights hardest, the one that will not give up no matter what, the one that sees only them, the one that is invisible to self to see, the one that is decidedly so for no apparent reason etc, etc the list goes on as we perceive of it to be.

For it is often the ego self that lays within the one that wants this fight to continue in an eagerness to be bigger, better, or more in comparison to not only others but of self to be seen into. It is in this voice of internal ruckus that one has lost its rhythm to be in tune within this that you are to be the everescent love of self to be holder into.

For you see often in ones demanding that comes so easily for it is easier to demand and fight, is it not? than it is to give up and feel of what this may reveal.

Feelings to overwhelm, I cannot see or hear thee, you could not compete, you failed, feeling like I cannot go on, I cannot keep up, I am not worthy, I am not desired, I am unlovable, I may as well die, does this sound like an option that one has viewed into or spoke.

Yes, it is harsh this we say. But in the many of you we see are to respond with comments such as these to be the one that feels as though all that you are trying into has become to hard. It is of the erratic fighter within, the demander to be the physical or the present self to experience as the one that compares and judges. This is the reasoning behind the thinking that one has lost the fight or is unwilling to give up no matter the demise that is felt as likened to 'laying the final straw upon the camel's back' shall we say. It is of this intregity within that the human component or form is deliberate to compete and compare in all cases of this life to present, *why we ask?*

Spirits' insert;

We speak the answer here to know; that it is attached to many if not most in lessons to discover in this that one is to succeed. All physicality, traits, personalities, disorders and dis-ease are to become the seeing to rise out of the main desirer to become as a mastery of this soul` self to succeed in an expansion to become.

See not to be hard upon the physical being for it is a learning machine, likened to an envisionment of a human earthly being that is not wise as yet to the wisdom of this great intent that lays unexplainable within, to be ever attached in a connection so bold to become of all this in a love of us once again. To discover your returning home, it is then in here this previewing or reviewing state that we hear you speak of all your learnings that have felt to come complete. Treasure the human that you be but go lenient upon one self as a human to see, for it is the hidden gem that you are to carry, this gem is to sparkle and shine into a life all of her own upon her voice to speak to hear in all that she is to acquire this time.

You ask why? To be more than another, to be more than you think that you are not. We say this here with great love attached, that YES to always be of more and want for more and to see of more is a great advantage to see of self into, if the ego is not the driver or attached to the wanting of more to be thought to need for one to feel happy or joyous in this self. In ones powerful mind that offers many thoughts to you in regard to your surroundings and of what it is that you are to see reflected back to you is this ones choice to value all opinions and how life is to appear for you to look into. One must be free of constriction and constraints that these scenes are to offer you, often attached to the thinking mind to offer his or her dialogue that goes only with the images seen. Be free to wander into all that you see, no need to attach a sound or thought, object or name to any that one is to see. Be resilient we are to say to the fighter that dwells within this one to be always to compare, to fight internally with this voice of love and let us say is often the winner until it is of this that we say, that ones such as you can look upon all that you see and know that this is you. Fully, completely yours to become, for you already are of this that you see.

Let down your walls of resist to become of this that you think that you are not, step away and calm your breath and thoughts to be allowing to feel as a quiet calm settles within, take another look to see that this all is just being reflected back out as you.

We are, you are, they are, I am all this that one is to see. We hold no intention within to be better, more than, bigger, richer, or lesser than of this that you are. We all are intentional beings to be found into to become and in this simple remark one must take note that you are all this that you see. It is the needy wanter within, the ego within, the driver within that feel to be the speaker of self-worth and desires of not what it is that one should be, but of what it is that you think of yourself to be. For it is of many that we are to see to speak of this as an endless, relentless quest within that never quiets, to always be speaking is the voice that is not yours truly but the voice that is unwilling to surrender to become just of this that is as it should be.

Surrender then I must? Are you to say?

What if this fight is all that I have left in me, and it is the only thing keeping me from truly giving up?

Giving up on what? it is that we are to ask.

Of what is to be so important to one that they will fight to the end, to see what of it to be that you are to think you will see. It is in this that we are to say that is where we see the most of you are to feel your demise. It is in the fight that you think is needed in this every day that you participate into as to being the holder of you in contempt of oneself to speak, of this life or anything that you see is not to be thought of as a challenge to be, for it is for you to grow, to expand, to express, to become even greater in the all that you hold dear. This soul of yours is on her quest and it is of this soul that is to often demand, for it is she that knows of all this that you are to follow, to reveal, to see into to become.

So, this we ask to soften your view, release your grip upon yourself to think that you cannot, for of this we say you will.

This struggle that has become a churning and crushing from within, is to be the holder of you asking you to just let go. It is in death, greed, unworthiness, or loss that one is to feel to be spoken of as in this sense to fight. For if we can only offer this to say that you are all in right to think of this to fight for, it is worth it to be. Is it not?

YES, we see the directness that this statement may be turned around upon us to speak, for it is of this loss, fear of failure, lack of to see and even death that you are to willingly ask of your innerness, your defiantness, your sense of soul that you are to become as the way to see this love. Let her embrace all this that you are to feel as failure, loss, grief and misjudge for all that you have judged it is of just this human mind to have caused all this concern, carrying within the stories, readings, and observations of many to observe and to hear of them to have spoken. Let all this that you hold onto as a solidness or emptiness within to be felt as an unwillingness to perceive as wrong or right for you. You are the holder of this great light that we see steady within and if you are to just drop the façade of this that you think you are, leave the human mind to waffle away for it to will fade upon ones ending to be seen.

Note of how you are to look. It is this that you are in this very present NOW, you are here in this perfect presentation of this extraordinary self to be felt. Release all hesitation in as to give up, for it is not to lose or to give in, it is to surrender from this ego holder in your physical form that you are, to be willing to listen to self-speak from within, to find your voice of rhythm again, to step out of your shadows that this fighting has so often covered you in. Let yourself begin to smile again for it has been a while no doubt, since you have seen your face bright.

Many masks are worn of this we know, for to live into this earthly life is hard and a challenge to be for most, the resistance, the fighter, the obsessed, the degrader within is to be the holder of you so tight and it is in these invisible identities or descriptions of self that you carry, that makes you dread this process to begin. For let this be known that they will not give in to you this heart, this light, this voice of love that you speak with all your might for they have been the rulers for too long it seems and if they are to give up, oh my lord what is to begin, what will be revealed... the thoughts are to wonder as to will failure set in, regret or grief, fear of loss etc all this is to compete within this that you are.

STOP! the struggle right now here where you are, let yourself go, for it is not of another that is to hold you tight in a sense. It is but this one that lives within you to be spoken of as the holder of all that is not right. YOU.

*Be this content in who
it is that you are.*

I have always been taught to fight for what it is that I want.

Is this incorrect?

Not incorrect we would say, but to truly ask of yourself this, 'What is it that you are fighting for and for who and why?'

You are to know that you are all the deliberateness that is to be yours eternally forever seen as this grand that we be. So, to sit into this place of hesitation to think that you are not, and do not have, is a place of unrest it is to be, is it not?

In ones uneasiness to find the love that is to dwell passionately within to be spoken of as ours and yours, is to be the holder of something much dearer to you than any who, why, what or item could possibly offer to you to think you are worthy to have of it to hold, see or be. In ones correctness to see of all that is in this real love[love of self] than they start to challenge this thinker mind and the physical form to speak of this that they must be, do or have as to be incorrect. One is to start to ask of what value is this to me. Why is it that I feel as though it is to be more worthy to me than a love so bold that is entirely of me?

Many seek outwardly, often this means a whole lifetime or eternity it would feel to some, spent searching and craving more to the ends of their days, unhappy and feeling unjust in all that they have not become, even if it is to be viewed upon by some as to have more than anyone. But you see it is of this that we are to say that the many that seek this way have not yet quietened their brain or their tongue to speak and have looked so far away from themselves that they have not ever tried to peek or turned to look at the internal spark that dwells within, for she may be dim too see and in many it appears as to be so. But know of this that she is always there and willing to appear if it is of only this one to just ask.

~ I SURRENDER, LET ME SEE ~

For in this simple statement to be made one acknowledges all their wrongs they think they see, know this of them to speak that they are not wrongs and are meant to be yours to acknowledge.

Be in a willingness to offer peace to speak for you have been fighting for so awfully long, searching to feel a calm come over you within, aching for a place to sit, to rest to just be, there is no other place to describe as unique as this, to be thee. You are the holder of this place to speak of it to be as yours is right to say but let us offer it to you in another way.

This place that you speak is all around, it is in exactness to be felt from not only within but in the all that you see physical and not, so feel of this to be yours in all that you see a willingness to surrender not to another or us but for you to feel the angst that you have become and allow it to rest.

Let the challenger be stood down for you have a commander that is much grander than this challenger could ever have been. He is standing within ready to command, for his or her voice is spoken in real time, as the real you to be offering to you this rhythm that you have simply forgotten to be. Let down your walls of anticipation to become or be not, for it is these walls that have, are and will stop you seeing all that is to hold you dear in this great magnificence that is you, this you here present in this very now to be spoken of as yours to see. Know of this now to be ours to cherish as well as all that you see, be present in this very now to become the song from within, the song that you chose to come here to sing, let her music be heard by you as the silent one that has stood in the dark for too long, you have been in the fighters ring as a deliberate attempt to keep the fighter within as the ruler that you thought as you. NO longer you say will I live this way, I have awakened to all that I am not and am pleased to see it as this and in this way, for in all that I thought I was not I have become this grandness within to feel washed with this love that is me to be seen in all capacity to be this that you and I are.

THE I THAT I WAS, AM AND WILL BE.

Patiently I have been waiting to be.

Not necessarily patient we would say, for all your adventures have led you this way, all that you have spoke and undertaken as yours to think, to be, to do, to have, has provoked you from within to be feeling as to be this exact moment of your so time to think. In ones reality it appears that one is to be bare to the seer to see, this is you the you that you have chosen to see. The you that has struggled hard or not, the you that has agreed or not within all that you are to see, the you that has argued to become, the you that has remained silent. Let this be known to you that this is you, the you that got you this far. Your journey was chosen by you it is to appear that in this physical being that you bare is you, your role, or your part that you are choosing to play.

KNOW of this though that in resistance lays fight, struggle, and dread, but to feel of ones heart to become open to see and ones voice to be kind in all words to be spoke, they will soon lose the fight it appears to the resistance of space that has got you here. YOU stand direct in the all that you be for it is of these stirrings from within that has made your struggle feel even more real, for all the unjust, the unkind, the bad thoughts to be thought are all yours. So even up the fight, lay down your gloves, let go to resit into a space that is committed to you. For in here is your life becoming fully loved by you as you are.

My offering to you.

> It is not to offer to us that one must feel as a need to be or do.

Let us say, we are always of you.

{My offering to ME}....

1 ask that you may take some of this struggle away for the fighter within me is tired of this I am sure to see. Let this fighter back down upon my request; for I am wanting to thrive in this love that I be, to know of all that I am so hesitant for me to see. It is of this love that I am to speak, for it has been a while this I know that I have even thought to view of myself in this way. Love, I say of what is this to be spoke of, for the voice that I have spoken many, many times to be heard has not had love attached. I have become dullened it appears to all that are to surround me to be felt as present within. I am in denial of this to be felt and it is for me to say that it is to appear easier to remain of this old way. I will let down my guard if you can give me proof of all that is to come my way, for to show my true face and to hear of a voice that

is not known to me is a difficult place to play. I am willing though of this you are to know, for my trust in this that I am to see revealed {challenging as it is to feel to be}, I know that I am a fighter to the death to win at no expense but this fight that I have been in for a while it now seems apparent that it has really not produced the win or the all that I had hoped that I would be to see, have, do, or be. SO, here I go it appears willing to jump in feet first, to land heart hard and to swing open wide the door.

I speak these words; I surrender - to something that I cannot see. But I will say though it is to feel of this surrender to wash over me in a way as to let all emotions and feelings be free to rise.

In this I will cry, struggle, deny, resist, and feel anxiety within for to feel as to give up on myself, this one that has fought to stand strong amongst most, she will let out a mighty scream, this I am to know. So, feel of me now as I ask of you in no uncertain way to utter; I AM here, and here it is that I willingly stand. I ask of you {insert your name here} to be me in all that I am.

In this I ask to believe that you already are steadfast, gentle, and kind, full of compassion, truth, and love to be felt within me in all that I appear. For it has only just been me in this position to ignore you in this time of human life.

Here in this my now. I request; I am willing to be heard once again, to expand and to grow in which ever directions I am meant to flow. I now honestly know that I AM this eternal being of LOVE, GRACE & LIGHT to have become decidedly created as SHE.

Here I am willing to complete this adventure to have begun so long ago and it is not of a completeness to be you but to be willing to see out this adventure that I have begun with an intent to let all flow. For I am not the holder of this that I think I am, or thought I was. I know now that I hold way more than I can ever comprehend. It is the love of all that is complete within us all to be remembered and this magic that is ever present within us all.

SIMPLY SPOKEN AS.........

UNCONDITIONAL LOVE

'I' surrender,

How good does it feel to utter these words, for it is of many that we see that they can hardly ever speak or hear these words to say. To have been held in this life of difficult, sadness or inadequacies to be seen, the many of you that you will feel these words as a release from within, a wanted one but also as a challenge to begin. Know of this NOW in your present moment to be that you are here NOW in this exactness to see, so open your eyes to the eternalness' that you be, let your heart feel you for the very first time for many it may appear this to be true.

Let your human chill awhile, to let the commander from within be your presence to reconnect into and most of all enjoy your smile.

UPON THESE PAGES I WILL WRITE
ALL THAT I FEEL I HAVE HELD TO TIGHT
LET ALL I SEE REVEALED IN THIS LIGHT, BE
MINE. IT IS IN THESE WORDS I WRITE TO
REVEAL; I ASK TO SURRENDER ALL THAT I
THOUGHT I WAS. BUT NOW KNOW, I AM NOT.
I LET MYSELF BECOME PRESENT IN MY NOW
IN HERE I AM BARE, RAW, FREE AND SEEN
LET ALL APPEAR EXACTLY AS I NEED IT TO BE.

To surrender is to feel surreal, is it not?

In the real you that you are, you are to know of this to be that to sense of self to be saddened or defeated in any way is to feel as rejection, or failure to rise from within. IN this we are to ask.

Who is it that you feel you have let down?

YOU......yes beautiful honest raw deliberate you, this that you have chosen so intently to become.

It is here that we see the many of you to fall, to escape the grasps of the ravages held within for it is this one to think of self as to be this that you appear to be not and is where the feelings of such to be thought are to dwell. Stop in your path here to be thinking that if you are not, then maybe you are not meant to be this that you think. Tricky words to apply when one has always been thinking as to be other than this `you. There is always another way we say, feel upon your paths journey to have become, has it flowed then maybe stopped as to feel non- fluent to you. It is in ones choosing to go the hard yards or the difficult path to prove that they can is usually the case as to why. Life is a struggle yes; we hear so many of you to admit {in what you speak you shall experience to see} for there are many obstacles that one is to predict to see and willing to place to adjust their sensing for this self to be. Life is an acceptance by you in this place to be the learnings and expansion that one is to see but know of this that we are to speak that you are the seer of all that you see present. Let this remind you of what it appears to be your observation of in relation to what it is that one is to be. You are all founded in good faith to become of this love once again so your internal knowing knows of this place and it is only the physical realm or reality that you chose to sit that carries within it a place of hurt, sadness or regret to have been or not, often this thinker within is the thoughts that are to heavy to hold or to carry for most and if one can flick the switch and be willing to see honesty as a necessity to be revealed, than they will not anticipate the next now or the next, they will just know that they are to expand into this experience known as life for now, to become all the righteous that they are to have sworn shall we say to experience in this want to become. We see many of you here in dismay as to the discoveries that one has made thus far to be revealed, for of this we are to observe that the many of you if not most are to be intimidated here to speak of all that they feel as to be not achieved to see.

We see you differently, it appears in many of you to ask.

Wanting to be is a right from within, a right that has been formed so intently from within in this understanding of self to become.

A right to what it is that you ask?

What is it that can be more than you to love oneself in all her/his integrity to be seen? Perfection it is a mastery all of her own, deliberate being within to guide and project this ever-unconditional love to be spoke, this presence within to be felt as right and correct, this essence of love that is yours in all that abounds. You see it is of this that we know that you are to always be the reflective image back in us that we be. Your growth is expediential in all that you appear to be and do, but it is in your denying to self your own worth, that lays your demise. It is to be justified by others and ones that do not appear to really matter, neglectful to speak and unjust to be spoke, you are viewing of self in an awkward way, a way for self-revoke to be felt as not equal to most.

Hear this we offer; you are to be seen in all comparison of this that we be, you are level and equal in all anticipation to be, you are the entirety that we are to become and have already been, you are the sensing of this souls unity within to be held continually in this big love, so let oneself feel to release of this, to surrender from within this that you see as incorrect, this is not to be to the all that we be, standing ever present in your light to see.

Stepping out of the shadows and into the light is not easy, we hear you speak.

When one has been witness to conversations of many that have been told and spoken to us in this way, we are the deliberate intent from within that is eager to explain. You are not to be scared or intimidated by what it is that you speak as a shadow of dark, for in this darkness lays all eternity to be seen, and here in these crevices of what appears to hold no light they do but in the depths of ones desires lays mistruths and no trust to see of what is really within. These shadows are you to be asked to carry for your interpretations of shadows to be fall into many categories it seems.

These shadows in a human concept to speak are doubt, grief, to trust not, self-loathing, disgust, fear, and lack of faith, they bring to the fore many issues that one is to hold. So, dive in deep it is that we say for they are not as dark or as deep as one thinks to believe. All aspects of self are worn and carried in this physical form for many have tucked and hidden away issues of long gone to be held until this very day, this now to speak of you to reveal and finally acknowledge or maybe release so in here {of human} it is that they may feel heavy and extraordinarily hard to combat but know of this that we certainly have your back. It is ones fear to see themselves free, loved and clearly that they resist and hold so belongingly to the perception of this you to be. Not wanting to appear in the raw shall we say, stripped bare by the voice to speak from within. It is she who sees you in this beautifully naked magnificent way, so it is of this that you think oneself to be never not or unable to hear that you will not hear her say,

I am sorry she offers to you in this way, this she you see is not and nor will she be. She is the strength of you, the light that beams, the ever-knowing voice of god source to be spoken of for you in the kindest and always loving way.

Humans are complicated it appears, are we not?

In ones asking of this to be as answered; it is to offer here that YES you are to be seen as complicated in which it is that one is to apply circumstance, suggestion, judgement, comparison, thought, analysing and categorising to all that one is to see.

In this it is that you do, for to become in all learnings to master and experience it is of this we offer that you must do.

It is of this inquisitiveness that you are to delve into to be of the thinker mind to feel needing to define, to label, name and categorise everything has to have a solution, or an answer does it not?

All is required or questioned until proven, able to be seen to comprehend, or believe, is it not?

We are of an approach to be spoken of to receive in this way that as extravagant in which it is that we appear to be we are of the simplest terms of acknowledgement to be for in all that you see and not is of us in this you that you be. We are not complicated in the truth of us to be it is only in ones inquiring mind to see, to think of this that we be to need to feel of us as to see. This complication that appears attached to the many thoughts and offerings that one has to think and speak is so often entwined within a suggestion of self to be thinking into as an offering relating to themselves to be spoke. So, to eliminate the complicated side of this to be spoke one must be prepared to just let things go, for all knowledge and learnings are from within so deeply encrypted and spoke from your wise channels of self-thought to be the innerness that you are as the one to speak, she has not felt the need to complicate this being to be. In ones choosing to be in this place of questioning to be it is to be spoken of that they are in need to be seeing of this that we are and to feel the need for the map of life to be offered to show them the way. Let us suggest; it is not of this map or guide book that one is to require, only of the heart to be the guider, the speaker of all that one is to need.

So uncomplicate your journeys to see and let the one that shines from within be this offeror to you to see to know of her existence to be us.

Complications arise in this particular form for you are to carry many heavy contradictions within with the choosing to see contrast and offerings from all that you are to see to surround you to be. In the many labels, masks, conversations, and sights to have seen, listening, and asking of this to be spoken to be heard are to all be in ones thinking to need to learn. It is of this exquisite being to be that she has developed into this very being of physicality to become so that one can learn to experience and evoke from within all those earthly perceptions of emotions and feelings attached. It is in the living of this life that you be that it has become the complicated version of oneself to become.

For it is much that has been attached to all thoughts and asking of this one to be, many deliberate interpretations have been accepted or inquired into to accept to find a change from within ones perception as to the who and what it is that one feels or thinks of self to be.

Let us offer that it is in HOPE shall we offer, that many are to seek and feel this endless search to be theirs to keep questioning of the many that are to feel as to be knowing of this that you are to be. Becoming the reasoning behind this that you are to think and are interpreting this self as to be not complete or hesitant to accept this truthfulness from within to be exposed as the ever divine self to be just right.

All partaking in interaction within all that you are presented with to interpret as yours to digest shall we say for this we observe often that many upon your path are always to view of you in a certain way to be understood as theirs. It is this to say that they are not the knowers of you, it is only through their eyes that they are to see you as. So, eliminate this constant quest or drive from within that is to see not of self as beautifully formed and intuitively filled with wisdom or rightfulness to be heard as yours, for it is in this lacking that one is to see to speak that they are to feel this complication of mind and thought to be yours to interpret as this that you are. It appears much deliberate thought and negative energy is transmitted throughout one's life journey in regard to the asking and questioning that one is to think into, in all searching that one is to undertake to find the best representation of this self to be whether by choice or comparison to another or in an actual revealing to find the real you.

The real you we say has been there all along this is you to be seen, reflected back to self in the image that one is to see. If you are not to like this view then it is to say that you are the holder of all that you see to be correct or not, so eliminate the debilitating voice from within, let your heart speak your voices of love. Connection is to be felt once again back into this unique being of love that you are to be a willing wanter of the all that you be to be seen as perfection in this magnificence that you be. Not a complication or err to be thought for in this thinking to be thought is where most of the maze like unfound truths are to lay, you are the finder of self to be witnessed YES this we say, but be easy upon ones asking to interrogate for you are to criticise and debate the voice of love to be yours to hear to the death it appears to say that one is not right in herself until all is in absolute of negotiation to be spoke of in this formidable way.

See yourself as right and correct for you have earned your stripes shall we say to be this being of light . You are the one that is to shine and light yourself up to be seen, this light is not complicated in the all that it is to see you to stand into for your light appears as the greatest asset that one is holding.

So, to view of complications as such, YES we say, many challenges are presented to you in many ways but let us offer that this is of yours to navigate through so be willing to hear and interpret of all that you are to see, to feel, to be and do.

In ones response to self and more importantly of others let the shroud of misconception or judgement of self to be thrown off for you are this perfection in this place that you stand, for all that you have undertaken to be here in this your now has and will be always the best of you to be seen.

Here in your now is where it is that you are to stand. Let all inquisitive thoughts of this that you be, be cleared to be seen, to be heard that you are this because it was of you to ask.

I LOVE YOU,
{my love letter}

From the depths of my very being, in this heart that I feel to hear, is my voice of love for me to feel. It is in this voice of love that I must trust for she is to be spoken of in all correct and right to speak. I hear her loudly from within in a voice of translation to be spoke of in this very way that one must sit to hear. It is to be of clear intent that this one is to speak for her voice is direct yet soft in all that she appears to speak. I feel of her as she utters these words of right within me, I hear her to know that she is mine to be spoke. I watch on as she speaks these words of love and not only of me but all that I am to surround, for I feel her truth in all that she says relevant to be shown as you and me to be seen as a completeness of essence in this that we be.

The voice that I am now in choice to become will radiate from within this form that I be, to be always speaking in this tone of love for me. I will not challenge of all that is to

be spoken of as correct for it is this that
I asked of her to be said, she willingly sat
in my depths to be cherishing of this that
I was to be, waiting patiently for my form
to be accepting of thee. When one is to
turn inside this self to be heard and to be
deafened to the outer world and its views,
this voice will become clearer and louder to
thee, instantly being recognised as thee.

You are this voice that speaks in raptures
of this self to be extravagant, willing,
and right. It is this voice that makes you
complete. Hear of her here in this your
NOW for you will never not hear of her
to be more correct than this present
NOW in these words of yours to be
spoke of as this LOVE in every aspect to
be yours to shine. So here I stand raw,
opened and revealed in this voice I AM.

I surrender
to her and all that she divinely
speaks within as ALL to be me.

CHAPTER 9

TRUTH

You have questioned to ask. You have searched to find. You have felt to feel. You have listened to hear. You have sat quiet for peace. You have spoken to speak. You have surrendered……

Now you must trust.

In the faith that one is to find willing and offering so intently from this one inside. You are to feel as this sense of safe is to evolve out of no where it is to appear for the many of you here. Many moments of your so said time having been spent delving into this one to know, to find the real you that you wish to be. So, here it is that one is to feel, are you not? That to hide of this truth no more you will not. You are to feel this commitment to yourself to become and agreement within in one's willingness to become of this that you are to see yourself in again. You feel without compromise or doubt that you are this to be, to trust this that you are you must. It is in a giving from the physical self to be to let go of all that has held you captive to see.

Your counterparts of seclusion have been unveiled, your voice has found love to be kind, you have resolved your issues from within also knowing that if and when of this you are to be sure that they may arise once again but to know of this that you are now to trust in self and the way that you will feel to see of these again. You are obsessed with this new way to feel, diligent to the one within holding you dear. Yes, it is of this that we say that one is to feel like a priest or rabi that has found religion or her/his god to be spoken into every moment of every day. This rush that is to surpass of any that one will feel in the reality of the external realms to be felt, is one that will allow for you to yearn to be of this trusting in us to be always a part of thee.

We sense in some of you here hesitant to speak these words of trust, faith, god like, love, peace and surrender for it is of this that you be to be spoken of by us in this way. You are the physical components of this life to be but know of this that in the deeper essence that you are to be seen you carry within you this magnitude of love that beams far greater than any sun, that shines greater than any star to be seen and that you are filled to be exquisite in this very way fuller than any universe, galaxy, or milky way.

So, step into this word of TRUST to be spoken of by you in this way. You will feel of hands that are to offer you guidance, you will feel of the heart to lead your way, you will feel of this that you think self to be, grow and expand in an awkward way, unnatural as it may feel know of this to be spoken of by us that we see every intent that has become of you to speak, for you are equipped within with this innate knowledge planted within that never is to second guess or condemn a trust or faith so grand to be spoken of in any way.

Your trusting is for you to decide but as you are to read the journeys that one is to travel is revealing in all forms of this self to become. Many times, and many lives you have been loved. You have found and become, and you will find and grow to become again, again and again for this is how you are to experience this journey of yours in this way. Ever received by us to be completed in this life that you have participated into as one to see of maybe in this space just a willingness to have been.

For all hardships, loves and losses, people and places, conversations, fights, dilemmas and hardships, extravagances and miracles along your way have let you evolve out of this one to partake in this reality of human to sense of herself or himself to be the adventurer from the realms of certainty is where it is that one began so you are the creator of this that one feels certain to become of again in all eternalness to be felt.

See yourself here in this your NOW, if you are to not partake in this that is spoke or if it does not feel your need to know of this that we be; this is okay in every way, for you are you determined by this innerness to become in this certain way. So, feel not as to disbelieve or negate of this that you have read to respond of as in any way. Know of this when you feel the gentle tug, whisper or even just a pull of disbelief from inside is sure to become a willingness for you to feel like a stirring that is to swell internally to be felt, maybe you will put all this aside and brush it off as just another story or misconception to be told, this we say is your right in every way, but just maybe it will open to entice you as a seer to see in a new way to view of this self to be. One not so physical but of a perception and conception in all that one is to be. We are not here to persuade, imprint or suggest to you in any way, for our forms that we be ever present in the all that you see are witness to be abound in every smile, image, shape, or shadow to be.

We let of you here to be spoken of all that feels just and correct within you for you are the dreamers, the desirers, the seers, the magic, the commanders of this exquisite self to be so let all that feels hard to you to keep as a truth within you feel be allowed to be evoked in your thoughts of not to be.

We hesitate here though to be a thought that you must know of us to be ever present in every expanse of this very being to be whether felt or not.

Request a different stance in opinion or thought to be accepted in just this one moment of your time and let us find a way to be felt within you, to close of one's physical eyes, hold your hand to your heart and notice this breath in and out to fill your physical self, for in here it is that one is to ask....

AM I WILLING? ARE YOU REAL?
IS THIS MINE TO FEEL?

We know of most if not the many that are to find themselves here to be thinking WHY NOW?

WHY NOT WE SAY, for we are found in the most extravagant ways often it is to appear, whether by thought, curiosity or words like these very ones that are to have appeared for you to read, this is how many if not most have begun a journey from within to be discovered once again as the greatest adventure in this life to be lived to be spoken of to be felt, for here it is that one is to trust in every knowing in every cell of your being that we are the truth in all that is to speak. For it is of our words that are to sit knowingly within this one as she is to speak for her soul has been opened and allowed to shine as yours will be too in your good time.

This time feels right in this we are to know for this one that is to be spoken of all that is right and correct within her as we offer her these words to be spoken in this her real truth to be known so that she may feel freedom from within to the continual asking that was once hers to begin to ask the question that is always the start to ones searching to begin….

WHO OR WHAT AM I.?

In this question to be evoked in all aspects of self to ask, one will feel this truth to be spoken of in every way. Know of this that it will not be full and complete in ones search to begin but it will steadily steer you along to be felt as a challenge to accept in this self to be feeling to be spoke as the way in which it is that one must go. The hardships and realness of you to be unveiled will let you feel to slip and wish of this quest or asking to go away. But know of this to be that upon ones reasoning and acceptance of all this that you be, you will grow, you will shine, you will never want of us to go. So, let yourself be open to explore in which to change your mind for in this new way is love that one has never felt like a directness to be spoke.

You are the holder of this grand cosmic magic for self to stand into and become of this that we are simply known as you in everyone.

In this we are to be you, equivalent in all that you are, be and do. You are this majestic loving eternal being to be, so feel united in this love that is spoke by this one, for she has journeyed far and long it would appear to be, just to greet her internal being of love revealed. She asked of this journey to unravel and for all that she has experienced to become her real. She is this one that we have chosen to speak in our words to be translated this way so all that are to find of her or read these words will know of her unrelentless, ever loving being that has guided her in this way, this that she has felt the need to ask as you will or maybe have done too, to see the way clear for a clarity to become in ones self to be seeking of this truth to be felt as yours to throw caution to the wind so to speak and let us in. For your heart is to hold the key to the door that opens in wonderment to see, let this wonderment be known as the all that you are is us in you to see.

It is in this grand love that one will be bold in becoming to speak, hesitant at first it is to admit but willing nevertheless, you are to be a fulfilment within self to grow a confidence to feel so connected to your innerness to be a willing component once again to feel of this love as yours to give. In this love many of you are to grow, feeling self-worthiness and non-judging in any way to speak.

All resistance to live joyous and brave is foregone to see and left to stray. You are of this great intent to become in this we are to hear one's question to ask. **I cannot be this that you see, I think a mistake has been made.**

It is a story is it not to be undertaken as a truth to change from this that I be to this that you say....

YOU are the greatest believer to be. So, let all hinderances to self be allowed to be reviewed if just for this moment of self to release and to read, if not to believe but to be witness to another suggestion to be offered. For it is of the great story that has always been spoke that one is to be the hearer of since birth to be, in this we say is your god in every way to be the asker for the many of you to sway. Great this GOD appears to be but know of him here in the universal love that we be, he sits within us in the voice to be spoke as your voice of god in spirit to hear, he is the entirety that you be to have held within in a sense to be spoken.

You are as we are of this greatness to be called upon as your gods, masters, buddhas, angels, ancestors, voices of love, spirit, and source, and etherical beings to be spoke in this way. You will find of us to be called in the right way and you will feel of this intent to be spoken of as you in correct and right in every way for here we be spoke of as this that we be.

LOVE IN ALL ETERNITY.

More to ask..... `Speaking with Spirit`

I desire as always to be MORE, to envision and feel these writings come alive with words of love and embellishment to appear upon these pages so that I as in you may read to receive the blessed knowing in and of this that I shall always be hearing of. To feel you here in this way as to respond to my voice that asks to hear, to quench my thirst for all in this that you be, the constant companion to me in just this life as it appears to me to be mine.

I know we have travelled together further and longer in this concept of thought as to have begun, you have been this treasure that resides within to be my ever-shining spark of this grand light in all that I am to impart, to be the coming out, the shiner, the believer, the knower, the exquisite, the leader, the voice within me once again.

Lead me eternally spirit; I know I have asked but hear my human words to radiate into and of this human heart to call to you to request of you to be always this divine intervention that whispers to my soul, that sings my song and allows me to be always in this that I AM to eternally be.

I call to you like I have known of you never to have not been, to be in always a place of certainty to be spoken of as you in me, I fear not of your deciding to leave, for I know that this is not a willingness to be ever requested by me.

I know of your LOVE. Let all fill me full of intent to speak to this GOD, this SOURCE, this LOVE that I AM infinite wisdom to BE>>>>>>

We offer; Be called to never another other than thee, and let yourself sing this unique note, dance your own dance, walk your own path & LOVE yourself always extravagantly GRAND.

>>>>> Shy not away dear ones of this that you are to receive to become clear within thee. You are the viewer of ALL that you are because you chose to be.

My intuitive spirit speaks.

My leadership within this that I must be responsive to, is the guider in me, to be called as such a word of variance by many but in this it is that I name of her as my soul to be the ever expressor of all that I aim or shall suggest to this that I know, I will be. Let me forever be in serving to this one to be the speaker of her words that she speaks to me to hear, so that I am to know of this just and right that is within me speaking of only a truth that I see as mine to keep. It is often in this entanglement that one would call of it to be human life and the perception of oneself to be that clutters ones space, so open your eyes dear ones in this we ask of you to be, to be always willing in an ability to become the most powerful being that you shall ever cast your eyes upon. You are wisdom wise and collected from and in many lifetimes to have previewed you by to be the holder of this image as you to be so glam to know of this self as grand in a way as if to explain of you this way. You are the ever wondering being of love and light in her ability to become the most in more of all that she desires to self {herself} as. Let this soul{this time round} express herself in a loud and defined way as if to speak to you in many different ways to be understood by you in a language that we refer to as LOVE, to be this expression that is yours to rise from within in a way as if to see only you as this intelligent pulse that beats so finely in-tuned to you, to become the listener of all this that appears to be spoken of by you. For you are the true knower here in this to be your ever glorious NOW, in here, this NOW you get to decide of what is it that I am or want to be.

In your asking do not fear, or be scared as if not to know for it is with a practised patience to sit into your sacred bliss, to feel yourself real that you will endeavour to find a controlled voice to speak this being as yours in your time of which it shall be to know of her well, hear her speak for it is of what unfolds or becomes discovered that you will be surprised to hear this voice speak from inside in a confidence that you are not yet to know or recognise as your wise wisdom that speaks to you in this way.

We ask of you dear ones; envision to empower in this being that you be to feel the intent of SELF-LOVE to rise on up to be a discovery by you once again to know of this that you be is in this entitlement of the all that IS.

NOTES:

Fill these pages with desires and words that are to unblock and infuse your heart.

Feel as these words of yours reveal to you in this essence that you are requesting self to ask LOVE.

Feel encouraged so that you may see revealed a voice that has desired to be your spokesperson always. Hear her now to speak in this time of allowance that you are to offer yourself to accept as yours in an asking to be felt by this gentle creature who you now know that you are to wholly, souly, truly, really LOVE.

....

....

....

....

....

....

....

....

BELIEVING IN ME

Set your intentions
Embrace this rich belief in self
Know it will succeed you &
outlive you, but never
out love or leave you.
No beginning, No end
Eternal to be always is THEE
See through your eyes of
Wisdom & Compassion
in ALL that you Believe yourself to BE
You are this representation
of the interconnectedness
of ALL that IS.
In Harmony and Simplicity
you exist as 'I'
defying time & space
with this Eternal pattern
in evolution to BE.

MORE BOOKS BY AUTHOR TANYA TURTON

Journey Of The Yellow Feather

Beautiful You Within Me

Angels Of Truth We Are

My Heart Speaks

Wanting To Be Me

Honouring Thy Self

www.ingramcontent.com/pod-product-compliance
Lightning Source LLC
Chambersburg PA
CBHW072003290426
44109CB00018B/2121